Mak Dizdar

Stone Sleeper

Translated by Francis R. Jones

WITH AN ESSAY
BY RUSMIR MAHMUTĆEHAJIĆ

Anvil Press Poetry

Published in 2009
by Anvil Press Poetry Ltd
Neptune House 70 Royal Hill London SE10 8RF
www.anvilpresspoetry.com

This book is published with financial assistance
from Arts Council England

Designed and set in Monotype Bembo by Anvil
Printed and bound in Great Britain
by Hobbs the Printers Ltd

ISBN 978 0 85646 397 6

CONTENTS

Message

ACKNOWLEDGEMENTS

I would like to thank Rusmir Mahmutćehajić for his support since the early 1990s in ensuring that this project took shape, and for all his textual suggestions. I must also thank Midhat Riđanović for his careful reading and correction of my first English text and Mate Maras for his detailed and insightful comments. I am very grateful to Brian Holton, who translated 'A Word anent a Son' from my English draft into Scots, and for his feedback on other translations. And to Chris Agee and Peter Jay, for their encouragement throughout.

The translations and Afterwords are revised from those published in the bilingual *Kameni spavač / Stone Sleeper* (Sarajevo: Kuća bosanska, 1999). Earlier versions of several poems also appeared in the following sources:

Scar on the Stone, ed. Chris Agee, Newcastle: Bloodaxe, 1998: A Text about a Country, A Word on Man, Recognition, A Text about a Hunt, Sun, Moon, A Text about Time, Rain, The Rightwise, A Text on a Watershed, Kolo of Sorrow, Radimlja, Cossara, Gorchin, A Text about the Five.
Why Bosnia?, ed. Rabia Ali and Lawrence Lifschutz, Stony Creek, CT: Pamphleteer's Press, 1993: Roads, A Word on Man.
Out of Yugoslavia: North Dakota Quarterly 61/1, 1993: A Text about a Hunt, Sun.
Stone Soup 3, 1997: A Word on Heaven.
Stone Speaker: Medieval Tombs, Landscape and Bosnian Identity in the Poetry of Mak Dizdar, ed. Amila Buturović, New York: Palgrave, 2002: Roads, A Text about a Hunt, The Gate, Wedding, A Text about the Five, A Text about a Leaving, Cossara, Gorchin, Message.

F. R. J.

Introduction

MAK DIZDAR was born in 1917, in Bosnia-Herzegovina (Bosnia for short). This was then part of Austria-Hungary, but soon became absorbed into the new state of Yugoslavia. In World War II, Dizdar was a member of Tito's Communist anti-Nazi resistance. Along with poets such as Vasko Popa and Ivan V. Lalić, he came to prominence in the 1950s, during the creative upsurge which followed the removal of Communist Party control of literature. Dizdar's masterwork *Kameni spavač* ('Stone Sleeper') appeared in various editions between 1967 and 1973, the year after his death.

For most readers of Serbo-Croat (now known as Bosnian, Croatian or Serbian) Dizdar is a poet of European stature. *Kameni spavač* is revered by many Bosnians for its poetic power, but also for its portrayal of Bosnia as a land of cussed resisters 'that wakes from sleep sir / With a defiant sneer'. The very specialness of Dizdar's verse, however, has made him resistant to translation: this, in fact, is Dizdar's first book-length translation outside the ex-Yugoslav region.

One reason is *Kameni spavač*'s theme, which is rooted in Dizdar's homeland. Its poems are a three-way dialogue between the modern poet, the medieval Christian heretics awaiting Judgement Day beneath their enigmatically-carved tombstones, and the heretic-hunters of the established Church (see my Afterword 'Seeking the Sleepers', pp. 111 ff., for details). Yet beneath the local, Dizdar explores universal issues. Such as the value of resistance, though it might be futile; of faith, though it might be illusory; and of life, though it ends in death. And the impossibility of knowing whose future is true: the heretic who trusts in a just afterlife, or the poet who fears an unending *kolo* dance of resistance and repression.

Kameni spavač's poetic texture is rich and strange. Dizdar uses a wide array of verse-forms, from the six-syllable folk-ballad lines in 'The Rightwise', for example, to Dizdar's own trademark triangular stanzas in 'A Text about a Hunt'. These are bound by internal rhyme and word-play into incantations where honed form is inseparable from haunting content.

Dizdar also speaks in a range of voices. The heretics use the medieval Bosnian of their holy books and tombstone epitaphs, whereas modern standard Serbo-Croat gives the modern view. When the medieval knight is certain that he died 'for his faithfullnesse / Unto his lorde', for example, the modern historian replies that the lord's 'deed was faithless / And his name was evil'. And Bosnian dialect stresses the local.

All this sets the translator considerable challenges. Linguistically and poetically, it took me twenty years to produce a first English version, starting as a post-graduate student in 1970s Sarajevo and finishing just after Bosnia's traumatic 1990s independence war. Culturally, Dizdar's world is unfamiliar. And his rhymes and medieval voices risk reminding English-language readers of nineteenth-century poetic diction, which makes it hard to appreciate how innovative his style first seemed to Yugoslav readers. But the joy of reading foreign poetry is that it brings in the new, that its literary dynamism opens rather than confirms our poetic horizons. This is why I am happy that readers outside Bosnia can now read this translation, updated from the 1999 bilingual version published in Sarajevo.

Translated poetry, of course, cannot reproduce both meaning and form exactly. My aim has been to stay true to Dizdar's imagery whilst finding him an English voice. If this sometimes meant bending surface semantics, so be it – better this than losing the poetry.

Translating, Walter Benjamin wrote, gives literary works an 'afterlife'. In Dizdar's original, themes of persecution and resistance allude to fascist-inspired interethnic slaughter and partisan resistance in World War II Bosnia. But as its English afterlife took shape during Bosnia's 1992–1995 war, when many felt that the *kolo* of persecution and resistance was being danced again, this added another layer of meaning. This is explored in 'Seeking the Sleepers', which uses my experience of Bosnia from 1978 to 1993 as a way into the story of *Stone Sleeper*. Rusmir Mahmutćehajić's essay 'The Text Beneath the Text' (pp. 127 ff.) explores another aspect of *Stone Sleeper*'s afterlife: the esoteric substrate of *Stone Sleeper*, which can only be addressed now that atheism and communism are no longer the only publicly-permitted philosophies. And by revealing a Bosnian spirituality that spans Christianity and Islam, it provides an antidote to the use of pseudo-religious totems to create ethnic divisions, which proved so poisonous in the 1990s.

Stone Sleeper tells not only of persecution and the passing that comes to us all, but of spiritual strength and simple joy in living. Hence we must not just be mindful of Bosnia's past, but also celebrate its contribution to world culture. Hopefully this translation will help us do that.

FRANCIS R. JONES
Northumberland, 2008

Roads

ROADS

You've decreed me not to be cost what may
You surge You charge towards me
With cries of grief and joy
Cleansing and destroying
Everything in
Your way

You've decided to root me out at any price
But nowhere will you find
The real road
To me

For
The hewn-out route the trodden track
Are the only roads you know
(Yet these are really futile and small
No matter how weary and long
They seem
To you
So proud
And
Strong)

You only know the roads
That start
From eyes
And
Heart

But that's not all

There are roads unfolding before us
That have no beaten track
No almanac
No departure time
Or tide

Your path towards me poor though I be
Seems sure and tried
In your sight
The sort that comes
From left
Or
Right

You fool yourself I can be found
By setting your course
For north
Or
South

But that's not all

Plague
Is wise
It seeks my eyes
Beneath the rye which ripples in the wind
Between earth's roots where darkness has congealed

And from measureless heights
Night's
Hag
Might
Press the

Strongest
Breast

But that's not all

You don't know the right of way
At the cross-roads
Of night
And day

But that's not all

For you know least that in your life
The one true war
The hardest strife
Is at your very
Core

So you don't know that you're the least
Of my legion
Of
Great
Evils

You don't know who
You've taken on

You know nothing about this road-map of mine

You don't know that the road from you to me
Isn't the same as the road
From me
To you

You know nothing about my wealth
Hidden from your mighty eyes
(You don't know that fate
Has deemed
And dealt me
Much more
Than
You
Surmise)

You've decided to root me out at any price
But nowhere will you find the real road
To me

(I understand you:
You're a man in just one space and time
Alive just here and now
You don't know about the boundless
Space of time
In which I exist
Present
From a distant yesterday
To a distant tomorrow
Thinking
Of you

But that's not all)

A Word on Man

FIRST

Born in a body barred in with veins
Dreaming that seven heavens descend

Barred in a heart bound into brains
Dreaming the sun in dark without end

Bound in your skin ground into bones
Where is the bridge

To heaven's thrones?

SECOND

Barred in a ribcage of silver your chains
Be ye so mighty no whiter than serf

Born in a body barred in with veins
Dreaming a union of heaven and earth

Cast out of heaven you thirst wine and bread
When will your home

Be your homeland instead?

THIRD

Barred in with bones woven in flesh
Soon will your bones poke through this mesh

Cast out of heaven you crave wine and bread
Stone and smoke's all you get instead

I see your one hand but where is the other
Was it lifted

To kill its brother?

FOURTH

Barred in a heart bound in a brain
Black your cave the sun you crave

Dreaming of heaven near once again
Your body it weaves drunken through leaves

Bound into blood eaten by roots
In this kolo of sorrow

Do you lead
Or follow?

FIFTH

In this kolo of sorrow not leader not led
You're a tavern of carrion a maggots' bed

Robbed from its body the tomb acts alone
But when will this body

Be an act of its own?

A Word on Heaven

THE RIGHTWISE

He walked through this our earth
Through night and through the light
He saw its wickedness
He saw its sick and maimed

And hee did hele them hale

And then he raised his head
To heaven he spoke a word
He begged the truth be said
About this graveward road

He begged the truth be said

The soundlessness of ledd
Did fille the welkins bowle
And they which heard his wordes
Were those withouten soule

And they which heard his wordes

The dragon the old snake
Laughed loud to see this strife
And soon the word was lost
In the unhearing dark

And soon the word was lost

He sank into himself
Deep in the catacombs

As hounds gnaw flesh from bone
After the hecatombs

As hounds gnaw flesh from bone

His body started on
Its voyage through the dark
But through the silence rang
A voice which fell behind

A voice which rang behind

A voyce which hyeth yet
And flyeth heavenwards

A voyce which flyeth yet

RECOGNITION

For in the deepest depths of death
                  the colours will be clearer then

A TEXT ABOUT A HUNT

An underground water wakes from deepest sleep breaks free
    and streams through a clear and glorious dawn
    towards a distant river
    towards a weary
    sea

Meekly tripping between the forest's golden green the fawn
    will not stop until her course
    bring her to her spring
    her source

Slipping between the ochre saplings the flustered roe
    seeks a vanished whisper seeks the fleeting days
    that pass between the dimlit grass
    that flit between the frets
    of grassy nets

I see that stag beguiled by the eyes of the doe
    entranced by her glance till sunset come
    his limbs grow numb
    his tread
    go red

A tall horseman masters seething spaces of unrest
    Handsome Dumb with deep desire Blind
    without a sound he tramps behind
    the baying and howling of hounds
    panting thirsty straining for the blood of future
    battlegrounds

I see it all in a second In this day's sun
        As if with a glance
        Of a hand
        And

I know that starveling sparkling spring will never enter its
                                        distant delta
        its gentle shelter I know that source
        will never caress its pebble of pure
        quartz

The restive doe will never hear the tiny cry that greets
        her trails her tails her through the cover
        will never hear the bleats
        of mother

No more will the stag climb the cliff and never again
        will he bell his reply to the green cry
        of the green
        rain

Nor will the tall horseman huntsman splendid in his battle-dress
        amid the cavalcade and all its show
        ever loose that battle arrow
        from his bended
        bow

For in that single instant that split second
        when rapt in self all were hunters
        and utterly
        alone

I Grubač the hewer did hunt these hunters down threads
 unseen
    them I writ with humble wit them I truly drew
    in the height
    in the white
    of this stone

SUN

A young sun on the run from his father
    settled an unfarmed heath between the icy peaks

Not knowing who he was we glanced askance at first

He rolled up his sleeves and ploughed the earth good
 and deep
    right down to her bowels right down to her heart

First he got his breath back and waved a friendly hand
    then up above the dark he soared just like a hawk

And he shone on every byway on every track and fork
    showing us his furrows and our faces in his rays

Then we embraced as if we could hardly wait

We came together became as one
    we ate and drank as if we'd always done

He wasn't just a summer caller this sun of ours
    even the barren valley blossomed full of flowers

All of a sudden our young sun stole away from us

Where he went to why and how
    only the good Lord knows that now

We might have forgotten him like some lucky chance
    (easy come and easy go)
        if we weren't still warming the whole of our soul

By the heat of his long-gone golden hands

KOLO

Hand in hand
        bound in a bond
Hand on hand
        salt on a wound

Earth pulls down heavy
        heaven is high
Were I a falcon
        then I would fly

PRAYER

I only own
A single prayer
Here on this

Our breadless earth

I've only known
A single prayer
A prayer about

Our unearthly bread

DEER

Upset because they couldn't decipher the tongue
     that might have let them talk with the trees in
                              the wood

(The men
    that is)

They brought brands and burned the forest to the root
     and the branch-antlered stags stampeded and fled

(And scattered to all four winds)

Heartlessly harried with hue and cry
    their sly quarry went to ground in hewn stone

(Which not even fire could burn to cinders)

There they grew a thousandfold and now their stubborn young
    wait for new woods to rise where they will live again

(Under its wing
In tales remembered from fathers and grandfathers dead and gone)

HANDS

I bore these hands like two banners
                                through fields of living stone

But now in the stone's heart these tired hands
                                are living on alone

A TEXT ABOUT A SPRING

I dissolved
And streamed

Streamwards

Riverwards

Seawards

Now here I am

Now here I am
Without myself

Bitter

How can I go back
To whence I sprang?

MOON

From the thick dark of a weary day the delicate
      young face of a moon appeared above our heads

Now he sails the whole wide reach of his sky
      waking those who have lost themselves

Before he tires of his shining journey
      before his waxing slackens pace

      (and he's swathed on every side
      in white and silver hair)

Carve his sign in the soft white of limestone
      so you may absorb as faithfully as can be

The image of your infinite pain and hope

A TEXT ABOUT TIME

Long have I lain here before thee
And long have I
Still to lie

Long
Have the grasses my bones
Long
Have the worms my flesh
Long
Have I gained a thousand names
Long
Have I forgot my name

Long have I lain here before thee
And long have I
Still to lie

RAIN

We need to learn again
    to listen to the rain the rain

We need to become not stone
    and eyes straight to walk unwavering through the city gate

We need to uncover the lost paths
    that pass through the blond grass

We need to caress the poppies and ants
    panicking in this plenty of plants

We need to wash ourselves anew
    and dream in clean drops of dawn dew

We need to faint away
    between the dark tresses of grassy hair

We need to stand a while beside our sun
    and grow as tall as our shadow

We need to meet our own hearts again
    that fled so long ago

We need to become not stone
    and eyes straight to walk unwavering through this stone
                    city's stone gate

We need to wish with all our might
    and listen all night to the rain the rain the righteous rain

A TEXT ON A WATERSHED

I

In this good worldes joyes
I Good Abel Joyce was ay good able to rejoyce

for in his short flight still he sought himself flowers
for when he fought and suffered still he stole himself stars

all through the strife of life his way he did not rue
behind the scorching sun he saw the heavens' blue

when time came to claim him he stopped he dropped by
    the way
his only destination the gloom of the tomb

now he needeth ne man ne thing
in his blue glade in his cool shade

now he needeth ne bread ne wine
there none be sated there none do pine

there no rain falleth there no sun shineth

no need hath he no more save one
to reach the havens of the sun

2

Pardon me
that I pray that ye

and my brethren my fellows my betters
do come to my door do visit me

I pray that godmother motherlaw aunt and bride
do speak my name keep me in mind pass at times by my side

for once I was the same as ye
and as I am so shall ye be

KOLO OF SORROW

How long the kolo from hollow to hollow
How long the sorrow from kolo to kolo

How long the dread from stead to stead
How long the tombs from coomb to coomb

How long the blood we are judged to pay
How long the deaths till the judgement day

How long the kolo from hollow to hollow
How long the sorrow from kolo to kolo

Kolo to kolo from sorrow to sorrow

RADIMLJA

Hand

this hand tells you to stand
           and think of your own hands

The Vine and its Branches

Present here is He
Who said in faithful writ
I am the true vine and my Father is the husbandman
    and Every branch in me
That beareth not fruit I shall take away
But that the field wax fat the fruit be sweeter the root
    be deeper
The branch that beareth
I shall purge

Now ye are clean through the word which I have spoken
    unto you
Therefore cast ye your brute
Matter into this fiery flame Abide thus in me
And I most surely in you
As in those I abode in of old as in those whom I loved
    true
For I am the vine and ye
Are the fruit

Present here is He
Who is ever ready for word and deed

Whose Word once heard doth heal
Whose Deed doth bite like white
Hot steel

Since ages past He awaiteth me
He waiteth and Him I surely see
I descend towards him down the line
Of this white
Vine

Sun Christ

Neither life nor death is mine
For I'm just one who stands in the shade
Of One who will not fade
With time

The black friars' fear
Is present here
The One they hanged at the sixth hour upon the tree
The One whose wonder dumbstruck soldier and Saducee
As the sun of His cross earthed their dross
As His arms stretched wide
And death
Died

Death sought Him out but she discovered nought
No bones no flesh no blood All
She found was the line of a sign
And since this hunt her teeth are blunt
Now see her flail now see her wail

Headless and witless and
Small

Neither life nor death is mine
For I'm just one in the shade of One
Who confounded death's craft
Who melted into a shaft
Of sun

I'm just one who's caught in autumn
Matter my bane my material chain
I'm just one whose questing hands
Stretch for the sun's distant
Resting lands

The Gate

Here just guests we stand out still
Although we should have crossed into a ring of light
And passed at last through a strait gate in order to return
Out of this naked body into the body eterne

When I happened by this evening late
Unbidden He said unto me

I am that gate and at it enter into Me as I now into thee
So He spoke but where is the mouth of the lock where
    the finger of the one true key for the gate to the
    burning stair?
I grope in the grass I scour my skull for the one blue key
Seeking a path through spring's flowers past death's scythes
    searching for that golden door

I stoop through ants and plants through sooth and untruth
    I seek and find
But when I raise my hand to the lock who betrays my
    desperate quest?

This dark side of the door an ill wind prowls a foul wind howls
I forsake my sister and brother forsake my father and mother
    between the beasts and the men
To seek my essence my pillar of blinding incandescence
How in the world must I find that word
And what would be in the finding?

Unbidden He said unto me
Enter ye into Me for I am that shining gate But still
I wait I lie I rot I die upon this sill
And the wind the wind the wind

If the gate of the word is just a dream a fairy tale
Still I will not leave this door
Here I want to live once more
This supreme
Dream

The Garland

Present here is He who through my mouth did say
That on the evening of that day every island fled away
And the mountains were not found
For the time is at hand

And He did also say
That the great dragon was cast out into the earth

The serpent who deceived the whole world with his black
    maw
That the angels are gone that few on earth are pure
And woe to the inhabiters of the earth and woe to those
    of the sea
And the hideous beast spread his wings and hid the dawn
For he knew that he had but a short time

And plague and war and famine did reign and we did gnaw
    our tongues for pain
We gave our hands our warm blood our naked hearts
Desiring to die and death was fled from us
For the time is at hand

So forsake your father and mother forsake your sister
    and brother
Be loosed of this earth of ours and set ye no store by
    its flowers
Come out of the city by the east come out of her by
    the west
Build a city in thyself and turn thy face towards thy city
For the time is at hand

In this world three powers shine three pillars of light stand
    in a line
Sun and Moon and the Perfect Man are the forces of the
    macrocosm
He and the Virgin and Intellect in their midst are the
    forces of the microcosm
The kingdom of heaven is inside us so let it be known
The kingdom of heaven is outside us
So let it be shown

And all the islands were fled away and the mountains were
    not found
The stars of the sky appeared before us and the stars were
    smitten down
And whosoever be not just let him wreak injustice still
And whosoever be corrupt let him sink in corruption still
And whosoever be blest let him attest
For the time is at hand

Ye who are pure shall be scourged all the more and shall by
    the sword be slain
And loud will they laud the hour of thy flight away into silence
    and pain
So take up thy buckler and shield and smite with thy sword
    that harrying horde
Let death slay death that the one true life might stand
For the time is at hand

And whosoever will see let his eyes be unlocked
And whosoever will hear let his ears be unblocked
Let one eye spy and scry the coast and cliffs all round
Let one eye seek inside him till his voice be found
For the time is at hand

The Fourth Horseman

It is time to think of time
As we gag at death's decay her stinking slime
It is time to think of time
As mighty waters rush towards us
See them crush and devour her puny power

Lo it is time to think in time
For a wind a swift wind a dragon-wind
Shall swoop upon us this evil day
For time is a fire so let it scour us so let it devour us
Lo it is time to enter into this time
Because it hath but a short time
And time shall be no longer

BBBB

I

A word is the image of a world we see and do not see
Some words we acclaim but some give us shame
Some words come to stay and some hie away
Words all have their colours and smells
Some words have a tongue
And some
Are dumb

One word slight and frail
Is scaling the slender rays of gold
Nimble and bold
As a little snail
Climbing from the hungry stone
Up to the sun-bush
Up to the one
True sun

Another word struts loud and proud
Right up to the dunghill's peak

We know for sure
It fills a space
But nothing
More

2

As if on wild waters some words swiftly come and still more
    swiftly go
Some patiently wait for the moment they dream
Some recklessly rush to let off steam
Anywhere and any day
A word only becomes a word
When its meaning becomes a feeling
And the greatest may
Be the word we do
Not say

The self-same word
When it enters the chest
Is a different word
When it is
Expressed

Words are everything and words are nothing at all
(And even these that I utter
Dust is already choking with its pall
And sweeping into the road
The gutter

And the dust falls more and more
For
Words wither and age the instant they're stated
And are ignored

By the rabble in the street
By the thirsty faces
At the seminary
Door)

But a new word is what we are waiting for

3

Their owners pile them like jumble display them for sale
On the heavy boards of bazaar and stall big and small
They go moth-eaten and stale
Like old furs
As soon as they're fingered by morning's first ray
As soon as they're seen by
The keen eye
Of day

(Only a few little words it seems are worth anything
When your sight is caught
By their sharp invisible bitterness
You find yourself fretting
Whether you're getting
Smaller
Or taller

But the hulking words of sundry theologies
Of bowing liturgies
Kow-towing eulogies
Are creatures of lethargies
Are creatures
Of crushing
Cacologies)

4

Words abound in everything
So words are everything but everything is bound by words

For just one word we wait and pray
An ancient word from far away

5

But we have heard a new word

Verily we have heard a word so new
That be it but whispered the heavens ring
A word which telleth of God's finger in the cross of the Sun
Of a city which shall be builded in us every one
Of a vineyard and a husbandman
Of a noble vine with stems which twine
We have heard a word which tells of priests and unfading
    garlands
Of a gate that is strait before our weary feet
We have heard the evil secrets of men in padded gowns
We have heard of the bloody bed which the black trackers
    have spread
With cross and chalice with flame and baying of hounds
We have heard a new word of a new a sharp sword
Of the wondrous shield of salvation
Which guardeth against the wicked Watchmen
Their books of lies
Their unsleeping eyes

A word which told not what we knew
A word which told us something new

6

This day we have heard a new word
A word which never before
Was said

We had heard the word about our daily bread:
The bread that is meant to feed
Everyone in need

But from this day let it be known
That we live not by bread alone:
Yea let the truth be said
About our unearthly bread

7

Heard by us here in the depths of this mere
This word was created
Purely to be
Debated

8

He spoke in a voice loud and sure
In a voice which no one could ignore
Through comfort conceit and drought
His words made the withered twig sprout the barren doe
    give fawn
No one had spoken so before
Each word was spoken to cure
A wound
His speech was soft and warm like the welcome splash
Of spring rain in a parched plain

Through the thick black dark on the shore
Of a brackish sea and in the temple
On the road and on the olive hill
Where till that day no golden ray
No song of canny cock or any choir
Had in it a word
For rousing a crowd
For freeing
One's being

With his searing word not with spear or sword
He became both reaper
And corn

His words hacked out a track
They opened a road
To the dawn

9

No one on earth had spoken like this
For he would speak words true and meek
Then he would speak like the slash of a lash
And wormwood and honey brimmed from his cup
No one had given us this to sup
Then he would speak like the slash of a lash
His word's very essence would fill us
With fear

At times his words would laugh
And then that laughter's fine gold wire

Would sometimes kiss
And sometimes
Sear

No one had ever
Spoken like
This

10

Speaking so I told ye naught of myself
That which I said was my body and bread
From another I take that word which I spake
Yea I spake only the word
Of Him which speaketh
Through me

And now we had heard a word
Like no word spoken before
What a blessing
And what a
Woe

For no one had ever
Spoken
So

For through him we heard
The very
Word

11

Here I soght me true wordes about the Worde
I strove to finde an image mete for the worde of manne
The word which telleth alle which streighteth us
On every side since ancient tyme
And alle that which awaiteth us
Lo I strove to carve a worde on the Worde
Which cryeth and waileth
Within us

In the end no thing did I kno
I wist no whit
With my poore
Wit

12

(Walking the allotted way between the dark and the ray
Walking the line of your sign
Assailed by doubt
And dismay

I come back once more
Crushed
To the
Core)

13

And so I'm still not sure
What my word to Thee must be

Hence I have only my poor
B and B
B and
B

    14

(Lord
Forgive me
That I only arrived
Back where I'd started so hopeful-hearted)

CONFRONTATION

Wind in the black pines rain in the marble's veins
From sick spring to sick spring the seasons follow their
    fated change
Through days through years through centuries we walk
    behind a high sun through the forests and rocks of
    a frozen mountain range
With night's hag on our breast with dawn in our eyes we
    plunge towards a brackish bitter-blue sea
Past the tempting traps of omens in the skies in earth's
    warm moss in bread's yellow flame
We name the things around us to witness our steps along
    this razor-edge of awareness
They're dumb in the face of fiery faith they're half-hearted
    towards the hearty

We name the herbs claim the firebirds lure the beasts of yore
And with this faith we stare men in the face we stare them
    dour and sure
We pray to boundless horizons and rouse the lands from their
    frozen trance
We swim unseen through the welling stream of all our yesterdays
In thrall to unsureness we stray through our short today
We ask uncertain sages what tomorrow will betide
And in so doing we call our real being between the clouds
    on every side
Though we only know those golden leaves from dreams
We search for time but time does not know us it seems
Time does not recognise itself in the depths of the abyss
In the world's ferment of voices silence still holds sway
So with this flower of silence let's be on our way
Knowing this ancient silence will silence us as well
Crush us at last on our green branch slash us and smash
Hound us into these bones ground us under these stones
When we know we'll never reach our hope our citadel
Then we'll passionately yield to grief's sweet embrace
Then let no voice be heard in that ancient stillness
Just let that bell of silence rise in me
Pure with old fire heavy with new sense
Like the wind through the tired black pines
Like the rain that rains through death's marble veins
Through skies that open before our eyes
Let it ring as far
As the stars

A TEXT ABOUT UNCHAINING

Where there be psalms
                there be curses too

MADDERFIELD

We've been waiting a long time It's time we realised
    how long
Some had empty hands and some didn't know how to
    throw
Each one turned to the same sun but each with a different
    fate
Some have grown where they weren't sown
Some budded bravely but never found favour with
    themselves
See them stumble like drunkards from old hopes to new
    blunders
Some carved their spit before they'd caught their rabbit
Some were hungry but the branch was too high
And we gave you a bird in the hand with all our heart
We've got black crows on the brain And to cap the pain
It wasn't us that let them in Besieged by time by the years
    that waylay us
Was there ever a time that didn't betray us
We tread a web of decay towards an age-old pledge
That's hiding before us all the more surely all the more
    wildly

Good-day we still good-day each good day till that good day
Past time's thorns and switches past wizards and witches
Our hands are still here but we still haven't clasped each other's
    hands
We're still not free of their sorcery
For we've still not found a cure
Except this ancient lore
Except this curse this prayer
Except from river to river
From Drina to Ukrina and Sava from Una and Sana to Rama
    and Neretva
Accursed be alle ye Divvils and hale stanes and droght-bringing
    windes
By alle Hevens Powres by Uriell by Raphaell by Epimell
    accursed be ye
Come not to this Shire which Satans mighte hath harried sair
We have no cure but this curse this prayer
But they declare our prayer is no prayer and our curse is no curse
Though we fight a relentless bitter fight with the Divvil and
    all his might
To free his bedevilled gains and domains
We hack our way through the great stars which ride at
    moonlight's side
Between stewards and lairds beside bailiffs and sheriffs beyond
    the beys
Through chasms and spasms through crazy branches and
    yesteryear's days
Through all our tomorrows Through all our sorrows Through
    gaping wounds
With a bird in the hand that isn't ours With black crows on
    our brain
Tell us where Is it there Tell us when Was it then Tell us whether
    Will it ever

When will we catch our rabbit It's up in the moon
    Here you'll never
Beset by time only flowing through us who through it
    never No one
Who can remember a time that didn't betray us
We pass each good day good days towards a good day how
    are you where you are
And all these cures have left us sick we've got no cure but
    this conjuring trick
This hellish spell this prayer we tell
And this curse on the cursed from many cursing hands
All ye Divvils accursed be Anciliash and Acomirash and
    Cernicash
Come not to these landes
But what am I The voice of him that crieth in the
    wilderness although
I was no carpenter no fisher no splasher of water although
I ate not of the limewood cross I baptised not with water
My hope is a finger in a pillar of light
My light lieth in that hope
With this faith I keep my faith
This faith which hath no name
It is in the good day to which I say
How are you where and if you are
Yes you heard it
I told him too
But he's got no ears
So there he sits as deaf as a host of posts
They hacked off his ears because he'd heard
Every facet of the word
And he's got no tongue to keep us from sleep
The Justice in his Court of Law judged that it be ripped
    from his jaw

But there's justice beyond that Justice and a judgement
    beyond his unjust law
And day will have no might
Until that day when there shall be no night
May the wounds of ages weep for that day may the rivers of
    wrathful love run deep
Through murk and ever thicker dark may mighty swords hack
    all the more
May all the foul and fair may all the poxy and pure
Share this wine to the dregs share this bread to the crumbs
As killers and killed share their fraternal tombs
For this song must be heard to the very last word
Or corruption will be our daily bread
While we live and while we are dead
And by our frowning faces may we not be judged
On our way to love we trudged
Through blizzards and drifts through blossom and bramble
    and vine
So come birds dine at this monstrous feast come eat these
    stone grapes come in flocks
Through the sharp grey frost through the vines' grey locks
Between my curse and my prayer
Come birds of the spring
Come birds of the air
Come swooping down
Little swallow
Cuckoo of ill repute
Migrant and stay-at-home
Songster and mute
Partridge blue-tit and quail
Let my arms clasp them
Let my eyelashes grasp them
Let them enter my memory

Through my pupils
Through the swell of this wave
Through this spell
Which I weave
For now
We've stopped for the first time
On our way
Knowing it's time to look time in the eyes
Time to admit we've waited in vain for word and deed
    to meet
(And let it be said in the end with the right measure in
    our voices
That if our cries didn't rise to the depths of the skies
At least our shrieking
Was in keeping)

You asked me brother you asked me blood-brother
What lies concealed beneath the madder of Madderfield

You've listened to my words
I've told you all I know
If you want more
Go ask the
Birds

WEDDING

With my death my world has died
An age-old darkness
Occupies
My empty
Eyes

With my death my world has died
But the world's world
Will not be pushed
Aside

Memory's white tape
Pierces the armour of darkness
Between the silences
Of fate

And through that strange pane
A deep new
Eye is
Born

And on my skyline I see the dawn
Rise from
Nothing
Again

There's a golden noon mature to the core
And an evening of toil
On toiling
Shoulders

With my death my world has died
But it will not stand still
Because my hands
Are
Stilled

And even the stone does not seem
Stony

Under the blue under the high
And silk-soft sky
Of Podvisoki
The King's Thing
Is
Gathering

And me with no hands
And me with no days
And me with no eyes
And me with no
Wings

And amidst all the pain
I dreamed that white
Wood-nymph again
And all my desires
Teemed again

Again she wound
Like an angry snake
Around
My neck

With my death my world has died
But even at its heart
Death is not barren
Or bare

When the green grain mellows the green wheat yellows
It yearns to be reaped
By girls

For the brave battalions
For the battles braved
For their beloved
Braves

For Bosnia's thirsty roads

Because these swallows are swooping
Across all her rivers from Swiftwater Lašva
Over the Rama and Neretva
To Lastva the Swallow
Above blue Lastovo
Isle of Swallows

Only stone-birds these birds here
Forever keeping
Through the creeping ivy
Faithfully keeping
The warmth
Of a mossy
Glove

With my death my world has died
But the world's flowers

Are here and now
On every side

On wings of smoke
On rings
Of sun

Between the sunplants
They bud and
Bloom

Somewhere between the banks
Waters trickle
Praying
For rain

Somewhere between the leaves of sleep
Dreamed forests
Sway
In a kolo

Through a trickle of late moonlight
They tempt you to follow
To stray from the way
Again

Prisoners still breathe the thin air
Of hope
As a cold dew
Falls on their bare
Feet

Someone rushes through his city in search of himself
But in the end
He's left bereft
Of his only city

I'm dead
Dead

But with my death
The world
Did not
Die

Once again the gleam
In an eye
Fades
For good

In another soft eye
The dream
Is just beginning
To blaze

And over the high levees
Over the nays
Over the graves
And their
Stones

Over the bones
That glow
In the dark
Like ever brighter lights

High and low
Elaborate
Wedding rites

DEATH

The earth is sown with a deathly seed
But death is no end For death indeed
Is not and has no end For death is just a path
To rise from the nest to the skies with the blest

A Word on Earth

A TEXT ABOUT A TEXT

And when we saw this script we'd never seen before
In front of our very eyes from far-off times of yore
A long silence
Fell between
Us

This stillness was broken by a voice that was calm but
                                        outspoken –
        No scribe wrote this text for sure
        It looks like someone
        Was trying to
        Draw

And then a second says racking his brains –
        Look at the right that might be where it begins
        And it's merrily flowing leftwards Widdershins
        Who was such writing
        Written for

Those who insist on reading from right to left
        Are wrong all along –
        A third one says half crazed
        And half
        Amazed

Look it's a secret text from the darkest days of old
        Rising it seems from the depths of our murkiest
                                        dreams
        Its signs are like writing
        Seen in a mirror –
        Mutters

A mouth
Calm and
Cold

The fifth with clenched fists and trembling fingers tries to hold
This mirror of clear redeeming grace
But it slips
To the
Floor

For in it that instant he recognises
His own
Ancient
Forgotten
Face

WITH HAND RAISED HIGH

With hand raised high to the endless sky
To the mighty signs around me I say this day
My daily words braided from the grave
Which halted me in this aching move
To magnify the pain on the way
To Him

Stop
I say
To the sun which burns my brow
To the earth which grips me tight
To the day as it slips away
To the old serpent with his flickering tongue

I say
To the aged bard
Whenever he visits my hands
And flames still burst from his glowing embers
Whenever he thinks me and remembers

I say
But nothing
Stops
Everything round me stays the same
Moves on heedless without a break
Doesn't look back On it goes and on it flows

(Everybody just potters away
At their petty pointless chores)

And the word
Said in this wasteland
Dissolves and fades dumb unheard

Only my scream
Is as solid as this stone of mine as steady and firm

A TEXT ABOUT THE SEE

What strange face do I see
                upon the holy see?

Whose face does that face recall
                on the throne of Peter and Paul?

That holy face is from hell –
                it's the face of Sataniel!

A TEXT ABOUT THE FIVE

Four men hurry one man on
One man harried on by four

Four men scowl and four men growl
Through the mire and through the wire

From his clothes and from his bed
From his drink and from his bread

Through each hedge afrom edge to edge
From the free to set him free

From the home and from the tomb
From the earth and from the sky

Four men harry one man on
One man harried on by four

Four count one man loud and clear
One man whom the four men fear

A WORD ANENT A SON

I wad haud silent like a stane
     wae's me I am nae stane

And sae forgie me that I speak
     this word that will be stane

They hackit livin branches frae
     my levin-blastit aik

They snackit his fair airms that raised
     his corp toward the hill

On the roads that led til heaven
     wi words that brocht him hope

The twa airms he spak his faith wi
     unto aa the sternies

They hackit off his airms and left
     two muckle gantin wounds

They left twa wounds that willna heal
     ti be ma lanesome doul

They buried aa the deid bar ane
     at him black corbies pike

Whit maun a kinless mither dae
     in this uncaring warld

(– – – – – – – – – – – – – –)

I wad haud silent like a stane
    wae's me I am nae stane

At least allow this word ti turn
    a waesome tale ti stane!

A TEXT ABOUT A LEAVING

In this worlde I lived long
My yeres in this worlde were eight and four score

In house much richesse I layed in store
Ne gan I ne moment reste ne feasted I ne frende ne geste

In this worlde I lived enough
Like an emmet in house I garnered much richesse

Now I must goe
To mete my ende

Here I lye now pennylesse
Left behynd is my richesse

A TEXT ABOUT A KNIGHT

He loved the grasses loved the birds loved the clouds
Loved the heavens loved the earth
Loved each day dancing
Like a prancing
Foal

Therefor he never ne soghte him deth
But deth was ay by him
Ay neare to his
Soule

Wherefor for his faithfullnesse
Unto his lorde
He was slayn
Stabbed and hacked
And torn in twayn

Ne in the daye
Ne in the nighte of his mighty fighte
Deth claymed not that doughty knighte
He fell in a rebellion
In a rising against the world's faithlessness he met a glorious
    death
He died many long years ago
He died but he's still
Not dead

Now ask the name of his lord

That his deed was faithless
And his name was evil
Is only
Known
Today

NESPINA THE UNSLEEPING

The Watchman watches at the city gate
And in the east a thousand Watchmen wait

By day and night no sleep the Watchman takes
Awake the Watchman makes awake he breaks

On bridge and road his waking watch he keeps
The Watchman never laughs he never weeps

On city and village the waking Watchman spies
And into himself the Watchman never pries

The Watchman watches all that we touch in the night
By day the Watchman watches our hearing and sight

A look and the black Watchmen will see you jailed
A Good Word and on their pikes you're impaled

The Watchman watches at the city gate
And in the east a thousand Watchmen wait

The wicked Watchmen ay wake ay wake ay wake

Ay-ay-ay
An the Watchmen wake
Cursed Nespina no slepe shall take

COSSARA

When the hunters hunt her through the thorny brake
With my hands I build a bridge for her to take

Though they drive her onward through each muddy stream
She is drawing closer strange though it may seem

Now beneath the sword they put her head so pure
In yourself you're tall in me you're strong and sure

Still you are not dumb although you are no more
In the sky her star

Shines like a crimson scar

GORCHIN

Here lyeth
Gorchin soldier
In owen lande
In straungers
Estate

I was on lyf
Yet deth I hailed
By day and nighte

Ne emmet wolde I hurte
Yet I went
For a soldier

I foght
In warres five on five
Withouten buckler or maile
Ay alle at ones
Gorchin
Was ne more

I sterved of straunge sicknesse

Ne pyke ne perced me
Ne arrowe ne slewe me
Ne sworde
Ne smote me

I sterved of sicknesse
Withouten hele

I loved
But my lasse was
Into bondage taken

If thou Cossara meetest
Upon the paths
Of our Lorde
Tell her
I bid thee
That I my troth
Did kepe

A TEXT ABOUT A SHIELD

To shield me I sought me a good shield

But I cast it away for now I wield
The good shield

A TEXT ABOUT BLESSING

... And that this be seene by alle men
to whom it toucheth ...

Blessed be every governance given us by our Great Lord God
Blessed be every governance from whatever hand
Blessed be our King and every lordling of this Bosnian land
Blessed be the King's father and our dear Queen Mother
Blessed be his royal offspring and every royal brother
Blessed be the King's blood brothers and their brotherly
    battalions
Our Prince Palatine who governs the court for our blessed King
    and Lord
And Bosnia's Grand Voyvode for the wars great and small he
    has warred
Blessed be our Procurator Fiscal and the Captain of the Royal
    Guard
Our Clan Chieftain the Lord High Steward and each noble boyar
Each prince each duke each earl
Each governor sheriff and laird
Each taxman and exciseman each bailiff each Master of the Hunt
And every nomad headman blessed be first of all
Blessed be all our parasitic lords great and small
Blessed be their sisters
Their aunts and wives
Blessed be their scions both boys and girls
Blessed be their sisters and brothers in law
And blessed be their clansmen too
Blessed be our landlords and landlordlings
Blessed be our betters I say however many there be
And blessed be the scribe who pens each blessed decree

Blessed be his brothers in office
And every officer of the shire

And from this high table of blessings may some morsels
    remain for me still –
So I may bless beside all the rest our headman and squire
And all these blessings may be shared
With shrewdness
And skill

A TEXT ABOUT HOPE

And here is written
A prisonner which rejoyceth not

May he be the last prisoner
Whom hope forgot

UNWILLING WARRIOR

This old head has lived through many a war
From the hills of the north to the south sea's shore

And glory wreathed it everywhere
To the horn and sackbut's warring blare

In a single battle I caught two wounds
But they healed my wounds with a flower's juice

Until I lost my right hand in a final fight
And all my glory and praise vanished in bloody days

Glory like mist which rises into the skies
Glory like straw which blazes up and dies

To be given back my shilling is nothing new on earth
To be left alone on an empty road is poor reward

They whispered round me Nowt that's what his life were worth
They do not know that wounded I still overheard

Nor do they know that I will deal my final blow
To this evil fate whose ways are known

To me alone

HOUSE IN MILÉ

Our Grandfathers' House was built to last
In our hearts its strength
Was meant to stand
Fast

So let its doors stay open wide
For welcome guests and passers-by
And all whose hearts are
Grand

For all good people beneath the sky
And all good folk in this Bosnian
Land

For everich warryour in this mighty warre
Which is now warring
On
Warre

On all other plagues and all
Other rogues
Great and
Small

For all in life who ran away
From homes that got
To hot
To stay

From the great ring of fire
Where the charred

Stakes
Lay

From the twin gibbets of disease
And the hangman's high
Gallow-trees

For all who were burned
Because they yearned
For a sun that was big
And far away

For all who said
The right word at the right
Time

Even on the road that led
To the bloody end
The severed hand

Because of the word that bread is bread
And wine is wine
And water
Water

For all who bore the weal
Of the iron brand
On their pure
Face

For all who appeal
By the lawmakers' law
And yet do kepe the lawe

Of Goddes
Grace

For all whose only tongue was torn
From their jaw
When they would not forswear
The word they had
Sworn

For all the unjustly judged who died
Tied to the horses' tails
Between the twin black wails
Of two black
Knights

So let our Grandfathers' House
Stay open
Wide

For all who were cursed by the holy see
By Provence and Lombardy
By Zadar
And by
Arcady

Cursed in a heady incense haze
Cursed in the councils of crusades
By cross and
Blades

Cursed in the bitter refrain
Of Cosmas and
Damian

For all cursed twice and once again
Because they would not be
Grist to their
Mill

Let our Grandfathers' Great House
Stay open
Still

For all who do not care
For old
Or new
Tsars

For all who do not heed
Lordlings or kings or
Boyars

For all who do not need
Their wealth untold
Their evil gold
Their ducats
And their dinars

Let it stay open for all who do not refuse
To pay their dues
And do not abuse
Those who gather
Revenues

But openly accuse
And boldly scold
Them still

Let the door of our Grandfathers' House stay
Open wide

For all who in the Court of Ordeal
Have heard a Word
Gentle and
Pure

A word that was given just the same
To strangers in a distant land
And those who cluster round our skirts
Those who are close
At hand

For all the poor who covet nothing in life
Though life mocks them
From beginning
To end

Let it stay open for the unknown brother
And for the unknown
Friend

For all who are doomed to prison's gloom
Who are barred in boarded-up bodies
Because they long

That this word should belong
To one and
All

And that all should be brothers in the end
With this
Word

Let our Grandfathers' House
Stay open wide
At night and
Noon

For all who set out long ago
And are still wearily beating
About in the
Dark

But know that someday soon
They'll arrive open-eyed
To find someone waiting
There

So let our Grandfathers' House
Stay open
Wide

But if someone in selfish pride
Should suddenly slam
The doors of our
Citadel

Let our Grandfathers' House be dashed to the ground
And let it be smashed
In my
Soul

Let it crash in a sooty mess
Burn to bare embers
And black ash
Let it

Let it become
One great
Nothingness

And just like Satan's bed
Let it become a den of snakes
A scorpions' nest

(Forgive me
All ye whom
This curse doth damn with doom

But unless our Grandfathers' House be blest
By welcome stranger and guest
It will neither be mine nor thine
Nor our Grandfathers' House any more)

RICHES

(A Shepherd to a Shepherdess or a King to a Queen)

Lythe lysight lyof lymy lyeyes lyis lyworth lymore
Lythan lyall lythe lyrichlyes lyin lythe lyworld

Lyou lyare lydearlyer lyto lyme
Lythan lymy leyes

Lymy lylove

STRIFE

Once in good King Stephen's golden days
Vukac sired Vučihna his son
But Vukac came back from the land of Greece
With twice five wounds from twice five frays –
And so he died in loyal service
Of his lord

Once upon a time when good King Tvrtko ruled this land
Vučihna Vučić sired Vuk his son –
Then in loyal service of his lord
In some strife he lost his life
By the hand of Hungary's tsar

And Vukić his son sired Vukajlo
Wishing that health and strength might bide
He was wounded and died
By a Turkish sword
In humble and loyal service of his lord
In the days of Good Queen
Helen the Coarse

A chronicle by King Ostaja's scribe
Writes of such days and nights
Such threads of life and death:
Vukajlo while yet a youth sired Vukas
But when that his only son was grown
Tall enough to raise a sword
In the fourteen hundred and fifteenth summer of our Lord
Son and father were slain at the hands of their own
Housecarls and like two curs were thrown aside

For the fame and name
Of their lord

And this is how their pedigree
Is later recounted to run:
Vukas before his death sired Vukan his son
And Vukan sired Vukoman
And Vukoman then –
And so it went on down the line
Right until the present
Time

All in the service most loyal
Of their lord

A TEXT ABOUT WEALTH

To no man never did I telle
How I my welth did gayne

Now let it be knowne
That then
Into the Divils hands I felle

That thorough him
I for my welth was slayne

A WORD ABOUT LAUGHTER

*(As spoken by the minstrel Mravac
in Dubrovnik on the twelfth day of February
in the fourteen hundred and fiftieth year of our Lord)*

Once upon a time I lived and laughed
Swift my shaft they whiffed the waft of my aft

I'd poke and joke and croak and choke
Chaffing and gaffing I lay awake laughing

Well laughter was my life after all
I'd laugh a storm to keep myself warm

Then all of a sudden grinning was sinning
Sinful sinning sinful grinning

Then I'd joke under my cloak Behind my hand
What a disgrace Not in your face Contraband

If grinning's a sin it makes me grin
A sinning grin a grinning sin

And now once more the laugher can roar
Can giggle and grin at niggling sin

Again I joke and croak and choke
I lie awake and sin and grin

And laughter traps us in its gin
And laughter's din mocks laughter's sin

Laughter was my life it seemed
I laughed a storm to waft me warm

Unless I only dreamed
My chaffing and laughing

At all that sinning
And grinning?

APPLE BLOSSOM

Snowflakes are falling ever thicker and blacker like sins
In a life that's nearing its end

So will we still have eyes
When the apple tree in the garden puts forth its first white
    blossom?

LILIES

White lilies bloom in hill and coomb
In forest and field lilies seem to be talking
In hill and valley every lily
Seems to be burning

And while you're quietly walking
Between the blossoming
Flowers

Perhaps like me you'll think of those
Who've quietly walked here
Before you

Between
These flowers blossoming white

Wondering just like you
What they might be

Whether they might be cries
Of delight
Or fright

Signs of those who passed here once
Callously trampling
This trackless land
Of ours

In search of white flowers

KRAJINA: ENDING

Look a shoot is sprouting from the white stone
Sprouting from an ancient hand a dark face

From it a white flower has painfully budded and grown

And from its hidden nest a bird has already flown
Into the lonely ring of someone's gleaming dream

A bird has already flown down from its green bough

Can there be no serpent in this penitent ending
Can we really dare can this flower be there

Without the serpent's wile its venom or its smile?

Out of the white stone look a shoot is sprouting
From an ancient hand a dark face life is shouting

From a known stone a banner of faint flame has grown

A TEXT ABOUT A COUNTRY

Pars fuit Illyrici, quam nunc vocat incola Bosnam,
  Dura, sed argenti munere dives humus.
Non illic virides spacioso margine campi,
  Nec sata qui multo foenere reddat ager.
Sed rigidi montes, sed saxa minantia coelo,
  Castella et summis imposita alta iugis.

Iani Pannoni Quinque: Elegarium Liber (El. VI)

Once upon a time a worthy questioner asked:
Forgive me who is this what is this
Where is this
Tell me
Whence and
Whither
Is this
Bosnia

The questioned swiftly replied in this wise:
Forgive me there is a country called Bosnia
A footsore a frosty a
Fasting a drossy a
Country for sure
Forgive me
That's cussed
After
Sleep

Message

MESSAGE

You'll come one day at the head of an armoured column
    from the North
And reduce my city to rubble
Smugly saying
To yourself

Now it is razed
And razed
Its
Faithless
Faith

But then you'll be amazed
To hear me walking through
The city again
Quietly stalking you
Again

And secret and sly as a Western spy
You'll burn my home to the ground
Till all
Fall

And then you'll say these dark words

This nest is done for now

This cursed cur
Is slain
With pain

But by a miracle I will still be dreaming here on earth

And like a wise watchman from the East
Forbidding others to dream and think

You'll pour poison

Into the spring
From which

I drink

And you'll laugh you'll roar
That I am
No more

(You know nothing about the town in which I dwell
You've no idea about the house in which I eat

You know nothing
About the icy well
From which

I drink)

A meddler from the South disguised as a peddler
You'll hack my vineyard back to the root
So that beneath my poor feet
There'll be less shade
And deeper
Chasms

And every home will know famine's
Spasms

And from afar I'll let it be told
This truth of mine
Unerring
And old

(You know nothing about the sign
Of the husbandman
Or his vine

You don't know what such gifts are worth)

Yea my stay on this solid earth
Is nasty
And short

By destroying the true shapes it takes
You only confirm it
Whether it
Sleeps
Or
Whether
It
Wakes

In the end you're the hardest guard
God's strictest inquisitor
Blooded to the eyes
Desperate
Frenzied
From battles
For dead
And living
Chattels

You'll burn me I know at the end of the show

You'll burn me I know
At your divine
Your shining
Stake

Which
Is
Already
Rising
Inside
You

And on your awesome
Awful
Scaf–
Fold
I
Shall
Not
Shirk

I shall be steadfast as a standing stone
Till you have done your task
And your flame
Has done
Its
Work

Such an end will glorify
Your threefold cry
Amen

Amen
Amen

In my place
Ashes will lie
And for them women will vie

— — — — — — — — — — — —

But therefore after me
On the first stone cairn
A message of flowers will still remain
In blossoming strands
From good and
Bloody
Hands

When thy goal liketh nigh
Unto its desire —
Know then
That even his
Body
Was
But
A
Moment's
Home

Therefore thou took only his body into thy keeping

For that body was only
His prison
And his
Weeping

(How often must I tell you that you know
Nothing about me –
Nothing about my arrow and bow
Nothing about my sword and shield
That you have no idea how sharp is my steel
That you know nothing about my poor
Body or
The bright flame
That burns
Inside)

I'm waiting for you
Because I know you
You'll come back one day

(This you've vowed
By chalice and cross and blade of sword
Drunk with chants of damnation and incense smoke)

So
Come on then
I've long grown used to your ravages
As if to the throes
Of a disease from far away

As to the icy waters swept savagely along
By this night river of darkness that grows
Ever more swift
And strong

– – – – – – – – – – – – – – –

TRANSLATOR'S AFTERWORD:
SEEKING THE SLEEPERS

Guides

MAK DIZDAR's *Stone Sleeper* is not only a work of verse. It is also an act of spiritual scholarship, a journey into a period and people – the mystery of medieval Bosnia – about which no two historians agree. This is a journey which only a scholar-poet could have undertaken, for only a scholar can find the way to this land, and only a poet can understand what lies there. Dizdar's poetry speaks directly to the reader. But if he or she is to appreciate the full numinous richness of Dizdar's landscape, we felt we should also guide the reader along the paths that he took as a scholar. Rusmir Mahmutćehajić has explained the universal spiritual meaning of the signs in Dizdar's landscape. But many landmarks familiar to the Bosnian reader, such as the stone sleepers' enigmatic tombs or their even more enigmatic faith, are weird and unfamiliar to non-Bosnians: hence I have added my own textual notes, as a guide to the surface meaning of Dizdar's signs.

As Professor Mahmutćehajić powerfully points out, only recently has it been possible in Bosnia to declare publicly the true spiritual meaning of Dizdar's landscape, its fusion of Islamic and Christian esoteric symbolism. The same is true for the fact that Dizdar's poetic exploration of a medieval past had painfully recent echoes. In the Second World War, as a partisan in Tito's army, he saw at first hand the ravages of those who murdered and burned in the name of racial and religious purity, just as the heretic-hunters had harried the impure of faith centuries before. And this was not to be their last return, as our own dark decade knows all too bitterly.

Therefore I feel that I must begin by telling my own journey: as a student in Tito's Yugoslavia, searching for the traces of the stone sleepers in a landscape that the latest heretic-killers, driven by the same incomprehending hate as their medieval forebears, have since done their best to destroy.

1978

Students escaping the smog of Sarajevo, we stepped out into the little valley town late in the afternoon. The driver snapped off the skirling pop-kolo, climbed down the coach steps and headed cafewards. Quiet − flowering lime trees round the square, the rush of a river over a weir.

Just beyond it, N had promised us the finest mosque in the Balkans. Which turned out to be a small, white, empty, perfect cube topped by a perfect white hemisphere, its interior picked out in mock-solemn green and red patterns of interwoven vines heavy with grapes. Outside − chestnut trees, the fruit spiky and green, and cheerful, turbaned gravestones. I leant with R, my English room-mate, over the bridge as we left, spotting trout against the shingle. N joined us. 'Nice place to be buried,' I quipped. She smiled briefly. 'You know what happened in the war? Here they threw the Muslims in the river.' 'Who did?' She shrugged. And then we noticed the inscriptions on the stones: so many from one year − 1942.

(Years later, N says that I have merged two memories. One is of a winter visit northwards to the magnificent Aladža mosque in Foča, built around a sacred meteoric stone; from the nearby bridge, many Muslims were knifed and thrown into the Drina, both in World War II and the war that was still to come. The other is of a spring visit southwards to Stolac, near the necropolis of Radimlja; there, the simple mosque by the little river was all the more exquisite for being disused, empty of everything save sacred geometry. Somehow, over the years, the two sites had merged to form a single archetype, like the two images on a stereoscope slide. The mosque was now a place of the heart, not of the brain − which is why I have let it remain.)

Next day, the necropolis. It was hot; the morning breeze had dropped by the time we arrived at the wire fence. Inside, the *stećci*: rows of four-foot-high stone oblongs in the straggling yellow grass, some with pitched roofs, like houses for the dead. No guard, no visitors but ourselves. The gate opened and we drifted in different directions.

On the near end of the first tomb, I saw a vine heavy with fruit. Along its long side ran a frieze of crescents and crosses, beneath it a line of stylised, full-skirted women dancing the kolo. About to turn to see the other end, I looked ahead, and found myself face to face with a man whose head was the sun and whose enormous left hand was raised palm-first at me – the Uncrucified, the Heretic Christ? On the next stone, the sleeper under the stone, an armed giant brandishing a bow in his right hand. And his left hand again raised – to do what? A snake as thick as my wrist – no stone dragon this – slithered in panic half a metre in front of me, heading for the long grass round the tomb. I turned and sauntered in feigned nonchalance back to the others.

Raised to do what? No one knows. There are theories, of course. To ward off the evil eye. To stop the sinful, the enemies of the True Christ. Or in greeting to the stranger. No one knows.

The Bosnian Church

Even the faith of the stone sleepers is unknown. Medieval Bosnia managed to keep its political independence from the late 12th century until the Turkish conquest in 1463. Then, like now, Bosnia was a meeting-place of different faiths. Franciscan friars built their monasteries there, and Orthodox priests their churches. Followers of the Bulgarian priest Bogomil, who taught that the earth and the flesh was created by the Devil, may well travelled inland from the Dalmatian ports. Later, Islam, spreading up the Adriatic by the same sea routes, had established a presence in Bosnia's valleys decades before the Turkish conquest made it the state religion.

The medieval Bosnian state, however, also had a Church of its own. It is this Bosnian Church which is the great unknown, the mystery at the heart of Bosnia's medieval past. Its followers, who called themselves simply *krstjani* ('Christians'), were repeatedly accused of heresy, either by the Churches of Rome and Constantinople or by Bosnia's powerful political neighbours. But that is as far as facts reach. The problem is that no statements of faith by the *krstjani* have survived: all we have the inquisitors' tracts of their enemies, where dry facts are filled out by guesswork or garnished to make juicier propaganda.

One theory had it that the *krstjani* were followers of the Bogomil heresy, but this is now discredited. After all, a cult which saw all earthly hierarchies as the work of the devil is an unlikely state religion. And if the Bogomils spurned everything earthly, how could they have contemplated carving their symbols in earthly stone?

At the other extreme, some scholars say that the *krstjani* were actually quite mainstream in belief and ritual. Heresy, they explain, was simply the standard term of abuse for a Church which, like the Bosnian state, was becoming alarmingly independent of its God-given overlords. But then, why the Catholic Church's centuries-long obsession with rooting out the hotbed of heresy that, in its eyes, Bosnia had become? Why did they not simply see the Bosnian Church as schismatic, like the Greek or Serbian Orthodox Churches?

The truth almost certainly lies in between. According to modern Bosnian scholars, the priests of the Bosnian Church probably preached a moderate dualism. At its most radical, dualism sees the universe and the human soul as the battleground between two equally-balanced forces: those of good and those of evil. Pope Eugene IV accused the *krstjani* of this heresy, alleging that 'they admit Satan to be equal in power to

Almighty God, and hence postulate two prime principles: evil beings and good beings'. This is almost certainly misinformation or propaganda. Like the mainstream churches, the *krstjani* probably believed in just one prime principle, the Good, i.e. God the Creator. But they also seem to have believed that the world had already entered the final age foretold in the Biblical Book of Revelation, when the devil (Sataniel, or Satan) would be given power over the earth for 'a short time'.

But Pope Eugene may well have been right when he wrote that the *krstjani* 'regard the mystery of God's incarnation as an illusion, and hence that the incarnation of the Son of God, His passion and crucifixion were not real, but merely illusory.' In a similar vein, the 13th-century writer of the Dialogue of Pope Gregory accused the Bosnian kingdom of sheltering heretics 'who say that Jesus Christ did not have a real human body and that the blessed Virgin Mary was an angel'. The *krstjani*, it seems, saw Christ as pure spirit, untainted by anything earthly. He was sent to earth to show the true believers the way to return to God; but when His message was said, He outstretched His arms and revealed His true being, ascending to Heaven as a column of pure light. Though Sataniel's call is stronger, though only the few have turned their backs on his darkness and recognised the light of the Uncrucified Christ, the end is at hand. One day soon, Christ will return in glory, destroy utterly all of Sataniel's works, and lead the spirits of the chosen, the few, into the new Jerusalem.

Whatever the facts of the *krstjan* faith, the Catholic and Orthodox authorities saw it as a dualist heresy. And dualism, which claimed that the peasant's God-given overlords were actually Satan's placemen, was politically very dangerous indeed, and had to be stamped out wherever it arose. Through propaganda and missionary campaigns. Or, failing that, through Crusades which offered the righteous the choice of forcible conversion or slaughter. Needless to say, the armies of Bosnia's neighbours, seeing heretic-hunting as a convenient excuse for land-grabbing, were eager to offer their services here. Even so, the Bosnian Church survived almost as long as the Bosnian state. But the final blow came in the 1450s, when it was outlawed by the Bosnian King Stefan Tomaš in exchange for a promise of military help from the Pope against the growing Turkish threat.

This promise was not kept. When the Ottoman Turks finally conquered Bosnia in 1463, the Bosnian Church had already been driven underground, leaving no officials to negotiate its survival with the new rulers. As the Bosnians' own Church faded into folk memory, the new state faith weighed all the stronger. Gradually, most Bosnians turned to Islam.

1993

And yet each state must crumble to the dust of which it is made. The Ottoman Empire is no more, and the live-and-let-live pragmatism of Balkan Islam has no place in an age of terrible purity. Twice this century have the heretic-killers come again with fire and the knife and the one true faith, to harry the folk of Bosnia and Herzegovina from their homes, to drown and stab and rape and burn.

A letter from N, smuggled out of Sarajevo. The paper stiff with candle-wax. You remember the mosque in Foča? The Serbs bulldozed it. A bus shelter stands there now. Later I learn that the mosque in Stolac was bulldozed too. This time by the Croats.

Over the stones, smoke drifts once more on the wind. Under the stones, the chosen sleep. But the day they shall wake is at hand.

TRANSLATOR'S NOTES

A Word on Man

A WORD ON MAN (p. 21)

Balkan dualist beliefs saw mortals as fallen angels, expelled from heaven and imprisoned in human bodies. But they did not return to heaven when they died: their souls stayed with their bodies until the Last Judgement.

A Word on Heaven

THE RIGHTWISE (p. 27)

Rightwise is the original spelling of 'Righteous'.

The Bosnian Church knew two grades of devotion. The many – the 'Hearers' – were allowed to marry, to eat meat and to drink alcohol. To the few – the 'Righteous' or the 'Perfect' – these were forbidden. Many a Hearer chose to become Righteous when he or she sensed impending death.

More recently, Bosnian folk tradition says that those buried beneath the *stećci* are 'good people', who died fighting evil; hence the *stećci* have magical powers. Mak Dizdar himself told how, as a child, he took part in ceremonies in two of the cemeteries to pray for rain, and how local women would file stone dust from a *stećak*, believing that it would cure various ailments. Legend also has it that hail never falls on a *stećak* that is still tended. The direct inspiration for this poem came from a legend that tells how a certain Righteous One, killed in a heretic-killers' raid, lies buried in a necropolis near Stolac. His voice, forever pleading to heaven until his plea is granted, can be heard – but only in perfect silence, and only by a person who fights for justice in thought, word and deed.

The dragon (p. 27): depictions of dragons are found on *stećci* and on medieval Bosnian manuscripts. In the Book of Revelation (XX: 2), 'the dragon, that old serpent' is Satan.

A TEXT ABOUT A HUNT (p. 29)

Master Grubač, who worked in the mid-15th century, is one of the most celebrated *stećak* sculptors whose name is known to us. He is buried in the necropolis of Boljuni near Stolac, where in life he had carved a *stećak* with an elaborate hunting scene.

KOLO (p. 32)

The *kolo* is the South Slav round dance. Carvings on the tombs show that it has remained unchanged since medieval times.

In Bosnian and Serbian epic folk poetry, a falcon symbolises a brave young hero.

PRAYER (p. 33)

The Bosnian version of the Lord's Prayer – the only prayer which the *krstjani* recognised – differed in one crucial detail from the conventional version. For the word 'daily' in 'Give us this day our daily bread', they replaced the usual *nasušni* ('basic, essential') with *inosušni* ('of another essence', i.e. spiritual or heavenly).

MOON (p. 36)

Bosnian, like German or Latin, has three grammatical genders. Moon (*mjesec*) has masculine gender and therefore is personified as male, though in English we see the Moon as female. The opposite is the case with death (*smrt*), which in Bosnian has feminine gender, and so is personified as female.

A TEXT ABOUT TIME (p. 37)

The first verse comes from the tombstone of a certain Stipko Radosalić in a cemetery near the village of Ljubinje. The *stećak* also shows a crescent moon: the boat that will eventually carry the dead person to the after-life.

RAIN (p. 38)

the city gate:

> And I John saw the holy city, new Jerusalem, coming down from God out of heaven, prepared as a bride adorned for her husband. [. . .] And the nations of them which are saved shall walk in the light of it [. . .]. And the gates of it shall not be shut at all by day: for there shall be no night there.
>
> (Revelation XXI: 2, 24, 25)

As for the unbelievers, they would then gain their long-deserved punishment:

> But the fearful, and unbelieving [. . .] shall have their part in the lake which burneth with fire and brimstone: which is the second death.
>
> (Revelation XXI: 8)

A TEXT ON A WATERSHED (p. 39)

In the original, Abel Joyce is Radojica Bjelić: I chose to keep the original word-play rather than his original name. The first two lines of Part 1 and the last two lines of Part 2 are written on his tomb, in Staro Selo near Donji Vakuf.

RADIMLJA (p. 41)

Radimlja, near Stolac, is probably the finest medieval necropolis in Bosnia.

THE VINE AND ITS BRANCHES (p. 41)

I am the true vine, and my Father is the husbandman.

Every branch in me that beareth not fruit he taketh away: and every branch that beareth fruit, he purgeth it, that it may bring forth more fruit.

Now ye are clean through the word which I have spoken unto you.

Abide in me, and I in you. As the branch cannot bear fruit of itself, except it abide in the vine; no more can ye, except ye abide in me.

(John XV: 1–4)

Vines laden with grapes are a frequent motif on *stećci*.

SUN CHRIST (p. 42)

The *black friars* are the Dominicans: an order formed in 1215 to fight the dualist heresy throughout Europe. They were nicknamed domini canes: the hounds of God.

THE GATE (p. 43)

Because strait is the gate, and narrow is the way, which leadeth unto life, and few there be that find it.

(Matthew VII: 14)

Guests ('gosti') were the Elders of the medieval Bosnian Church.

THE GARLAND (p. 44)

This poem relates the end of the world as told in the Biblical Book of Revelation. The title refers to the 'unfading garlands' which shall be given to the Righteous at the Last Judgement (in the King James Bible these are translated less accurately, but more poetically, as 'incorruptible crowns'). The motif of the garland is a common one on the *stećci*.

the macrocosm ... the microcosm: in medieval science and philo-sophy, the microcosm was the mental and physical world inside man, and the macrocosm the outside world. The two systems were seen as linked or acting in parallel (for example, the orbits of planets in the macrocosm controlled health and mental states in the microcosm).

The Perfect Man: according to the Andalusian Sufi philosopher Muhyi al-Din Ibn 'Arabi, 'the Perfect Man' embraces two concepts: humanity as a species, the image of God; and those few individual humans who become so completely permeated by the Absolute that they reflect the Divine like 'a polished mirror'.

THE FOURTH HORSEMAN (p. 46)

> And when he had opened the fourth seal, I heard the voice of the fourth beast say, Come and see.
>
> And I looked, and behold a pale horse: and his name that sat on him was Death, and Hell followed with him. And power was given unto them over the fourth part of the earth, to kill with sword, and with hunger, and with death, and with the beasts of the earth.
>
> (Revelation VI: 7–8)

BBBB (p. 47)

One *stećak* bears only these four letters. Their meaning is not known.

the baying of hounds / the wicked Watchmen: the Dominicans. See notes to 'Sun Christ' above.

CONFRONTATION (p. 55)

Deacon Draželav Bojić was scribe to Stephen Tvrtko, then Ban and later King of Bosnia. On June 1st 1367, he wrote:

> 'The earth is my mother, my patrimony is the grave, from earth we come and into earth we go'.

MADDERFIELD (p. 57)

Brotnjice ('Madderfield') is the site of a small cemetery, some of whose *stećci* are exceptionally richly decorated.

The three-line spell (*Accursed be alle ye Divvils . . .*) comes from a 'Prayer Against the Blasts of Thunder and the Ravages of Hail', written down at the end of the 15th century. The text of this prayer shows that its users, though they had converted to Islam and taken Islamic names, still held to their traditional beliefs.

Splasher of water: instead of baptism with water, the *krstjani* carried out a 'spiritual christening', where the Gospel was placed on the believer's head.

A Word on Earth

A TEXT ABOUT A TEXT (p. 71)

A number of medieval Bosnian inscriptions are written not only from right to left in mirror script, but also with the whole text turned at right angles, so that the writing runs from top to bottom. Some scholars have suggested that this is because the inscriptions were copied by illiterate stone-masons. This, however, does not explain why the script was written as if in a mirror. The real reason is unknown.

A TEXT ABOUT THE SEE (p. 74)

The authorities of the Bosnian Church regarded themselves as the true successors to Saint Peter and his church, and saw the Popes of Rome as the agents of Satan.

A TEXT ABOUT THE FIVE (p. 75)

This poem dates from 1940–1941, at the height of this century's first rape of Bosnia. To guard against the risk of it being read by the Ustaša or Nazi occupiers, Dizdar wrote it in the Arabic-based *alhamiya* ('foreign') script, thus making it seem like a religious text. Alhamiya was the main script used for the Bosnian language under the Turkish overlordship, from the early 15th to the late 19th century.

through each Y: the Bosnian Church tried to simplify the Old Slavonic script in order to make it closer to spoken Bosnian. One reform was to scrap the silent letter Y.

A WORD ANENT A SON (p. 76)

This poem has startling parallels with the well-known Scots ballad 'The twa corbies'. Hence I asked Brian Holton, Britain's leading translator of Chinese poetry, if he would re-translate my English draft into his native Scots.

anent	about
haud	hold
wae	woe
levin-blastit	struck by lightning
snackit	broke
corp	body
sternies	stars
muckle	great
gantin	gaping
lanesome	lonely
doul	pain
corbies	crows
pike	pick
maun	must
mither	mother
dae	do

NESPINA THE UNSLEEPING (p. 80)

The gravestone of the tax-collector Nespina (whose name means 'unsleeping') is in Sarajevo's National Museum.

A TEXT ABOUT A SHIELD (p. 83)

The shield is a frequent symbol on the *stećci*. Its meaning was probably religious:

> Thou hast also given me the shield of thy salvation: and thy right hand hath holden me up, and thy gentleness hath made me great.
>
> (Psalm XVIII: 35)

A TEXT ABOUT HOPE (p. 85)

The wall of the Treasurer's Gaol in Mostar bore until recently the message: 'Vrsan Kosarić was here, a prisoner who does not rejoice' – at which the sentence is broken off.

HOUSE IN MILÉ (p. 87)

Medieval Mile (pronounced *Milé*) was the seat of the Primate of the Bosnian Church. Stephen Tvrtko I was crowned King of Bosnia there in 1353. Under his rule, which lasted until 1391, Bosnia became the most powerful state in the Western Balkans – only to become eclipsed by the Ottoman Turkish Sultanate after the fateful Battle of Kosovo in 1389.
In the *Grandfathers' House* in Milé, fugitives from persecution had the right of sanctuary.
Cosmas and Damian: Dizdar is probably not referring here to the third-century twin healing saints, but to Cosmas, a 10th-century Bulgarian cleric who wrote a 'Sermon against the Heretics', and to the 11th-century Italian St Peter Damian, a fierce opponent of clerical heresies.

RICHES (p. 93)

Disguising a poem by inserting extra sounds (here: *ly*) before each syllable is not only a child's game. Several Bosnian shepherd folk-songs also do this.

LILIES (p. 98)

The lily is Bosnia's national flower, appearing on the flag and coat of arms of Bosnia and Herzegovina.

KRAJINA: ENDING (p. 99)

Krajina has various meanings, among them 'ending'. Its best-known meaning, however, is 'marches' (in the sense of military frontier zone). Both the Austrian and the Ottoman Empires formed such zones (*vojne krajine*) along their joint frontier, which is now the Croatian–Bosnian border.

A TEXT ABOUT A COUNTRY (p. 100)

In English, John of Pannonia's text reads:

> There was a part of Illyria, now called Bosnia by its
> inhabitants,
> Hard, but its ground rich with the gift of silver.
> No wide-edged green plains there,
> Nor fields which yield crops of much value.
> But rugged mountains, beetling rock-pinnacles,
> And tall castles perched on top of ridges.

Message

MESSAGE (p. 103)

The final poem in *Stone Sleeper* remained unfinished at Dizdar's death.

The Text Beneath the Text:
The Poetry of Mak Dizdar

BY RUSMIR MAHMUTĆEHAJIĆ

Translated by Francis R. Jones

I

MEHMED ALIJA DIZDAR, the twentieth century's greatest
Bosnian poet, was born in 1917 in Stolac, the main town of
the Hum region of southern Bosnia. Readers know him not
by his given names, nor by his patronymic Muharem, but by
his pen-name Mak – the pseudonym he used when a
member of the anti-fascist resistance during the Second
World War. Although he wrote and published poems from an
early age until his death in 1971, Dizdar is best known for his
book *Stone Sleeper* (*Kameni spavač*), a landmark in Bosnian and
South Slav twentieth century poetry. The first edition of
Stone Sleeper appeared in 1966, but just before his death the
poet presented the Mostar publishing house 'Prva književna
komuna' with the manuscript of a new, radically altered edi-
tion, whose form more closely mirrors the enigma of Bosnia's
destiny. It is upon this edition, published posthumously in
1975, which the present volume is based.

Stone Sleeper tells about the *krstjani*, the faithful of the
schismatic medieval Bosnian Church, who lie waiting for the
Day of Judgement beneath the white limestone tombs (*stećci*)
which, singly or clustered in necropoles, still define the phys-
ical, cultural and religious landscape of Bosnia.[1] In this work,
a voice speaks out again after centuries of silence. It is the
voice of Bosnia, concealed in the numinous symbols carved
on the *stećci*, inscribed in the decrees and annals[2] which have

survived all the attempts to destroy them: the heretic-hunters sent against the *krstjani* by the established Church and the book-burners of our own age are not the only dark forces which have tried to stifle this voice. It is perhaps no coincidence here that *Mak*, Dizdar's *nom de guerre* and pen name, means 'poppy', the symbol of earth, sleep, and death; and when the order of the letters is reversed, we have *kam*, the medieval word for 'stone'.

Stone Sleeper was first published in an age of deliberate deafness to sacred science and sacred art – an age which thought it had put 'superstitions about the unseen' behind it once and for all. But its creator's intense meditation on the signs carved on the *stećci* and penned in the few surviving medieval Bosnian manuscripts enabled him to descend into the innermost depths of language and return with the speech of eternity. For this speech has never been entirely silenced: it has welled up in all those who, down the ages, have borne witness to the nature of their own being and to their belief in the signs they see in the world around them.

The writings and inscriptions which survive preserve a link with Holy tradition. Their outer form is Bosnian, but their inner essence is beyond the bounds of individuality. In them, through signs legible only in the light of sacred science, holiness becomes a tangible human goal. If we wish to give voice to these signs, we need only seek them out and meditate upon them – for man, created for holiness, has everything within him that he needs for the journey. As Jesus Christ, Son of Mary, said: 'The kingdom of God is within you'; therefore 'ask and it shall be given to you; seek and ye shall find; knock and it shall be opened unto you' (Luke XVII:21; Matthew VII:7).

This is the message which unerringly guided the poet's pen across the white of the page. Through the act of writing, the poet became another witness to the primordial, universal tradition (*philosophia perennis, lex aeterna, hagia sophia, dīn-al-*

ḥaqq). And yet, though sacred science and its symbols so powerfully illuminate *Stone Sleeper*, his words were written in an environment conditioned by the post-Renaissance denial of the link between poetry and the sacred. In other words, we can only properly explore the relationship between Dizdar's poetic voice and the language and signs of sacred art and science if we allow ourselves to be guided by the traditional wisdom of the past. Only in this context can we properly understand the poet's role – the builder of a bridge between Bosnia's past and Bosnia's future.

2

In every age, the eternal Unity of the Truth has revealed itself through a different prophet. This Unity can take a multitude of forms. Thus the various revelations, whatever name they may take – Judaism, Hinduism, Christianity, Islam, etc. – are all linked to the Truth. But sacred forms can all too often become moulded into systems of ideology and government. Though such systems can seem to preserve a link with the Sacred, following them brings one no nearer to the Truth, for its transcendent Essence has been lost or cast aside.

For many centuries Bosnia has been a land where different holy traditions have met and overlapped. These traditions are based primarily on different interpretations of the truth about Christ, the Anointed (*Mašiah, the Messiah, al-Masīh, Christos*). Bosnia's geographical location has made her the arena of two thousand years of debate and testimony about this truth. Her history bears the indelible stamp of these different doctrines, the clearest being those we call *Krstjan*, Orthodox, Catholic and Islam. These different ways of interpreting one and the same essence have given Bosnia a unique role in helping to shape the world as unity in diversity. Their coming together has left a long legacy of argument and counter-argument about the nature of Christ, through which

His followers have sought in themselves the answers to their questions about God, the world and man. Yet, though Bosnia has become a synonym for the diversity of sacred tradition, these different routes to the Truth bear witness to the same single goal: humanity's right to salvation in Perfection.

In medieval times, the doctrines of two great religious systems, Catholicism and Orthodoxy, gave rise to an increasingly distinctive Bosnian approach to the message of the Anointed. At some time early in the thirteenth century, the Bosnians established a Church of their own[3], thus fanning the flames of hostility on the part of the religious and political systems that surrounded them. The Bosnian Church lasted for several centuries; and even when it ultimately dissolved into a number of other traditions, it still maintained its link with the Truth. The *Pontifex Maximus* of the church was the *Djed* ('Grandfather'), who was held to be the vicar of Christ and the descendant of the Apostle Peter.[4] Its members, the *krstjani*, described themselves as 'followers of the Church of Christ'[5] and of 'the True Apostolic Faith.'[6] But the political and religious dogma of their neighbours depicted them as dangerous 'Patarin' heretics,[7] apostates who 'call themselves Christians, yet do not revere the holy icons or the pure cross'.[8]

Painstaking research into the books and inscriptions that survive has failed to confirm any departure from the letter of the Gospel by the Bosnian Church. In the sacrament of baptism, which the *krstjani* called 'baptism in Christ' or 'the baptism of the Book', the priest placed his hands on the initiates and presented them with the Holy Book.[9] This recognition of the Book as the light and glory of the Comforter led the *krstjani* to wage a 'mighty war' within themselves, a war to end all wars in the world – '. . . that, denying ungodliness and worldly lusts, we should live soberly, righteously and godly, in this present world; looking for that blessed hope, and the glorious appearing of the great God':[10]

For you know least that in your life
The one true war
The hardest strife
Is at your very
Core

('Roads')

Because of their insistence that knowledge of God should come through knowledge of the self, the *krstjani* repeatedly became the targets of murderous crusades by the armies of church and state, but they were never destroyed. This was just one manifestation of a struggle that has defined the history of Bosnia: the struggle between a savage external enemy ravaging with fire and the sword, and an inner power and resilience stemming from her unshakeable unity of being.

3

What, then, is the nature of the sacred science that underlies both the faith of the *krstjani* and Dizdar's work? A key term in sacred science is Intellect. Although the term has acquired many different interpretations in various systems of knowledge (and its opposite), the meaning of Intellect in sacred science is clear and simple. It signifies pure Mind, neither bounded by rational thought nor bound to any particular individual. Intellect is oneness. But as long as the illusion of separation persists deep in every creature, Intellect must be represented by three different aspects. The first is *Divine Intellect*: this is pure Light and action. The second is *Cosmic Intellect*: this is the mirror and receptacle of God, and Light as perceived by man. The third is *Human Intellect*: this is the mirror of the first two aspects, and Light as perceived by the individual soul. Intellect works in two complementary ways: it distinguishes between externals in order to unite the internal.[11]

Intellect preceded the creation of heaven, earth, man, and all else. This primacy brings it closest to God; but it also lies behind all individual forms. Hence, of all things, Intellect can be seen as that which is most imbued with the Uncreated. As Intellect lies above all created things, it is reflected in them all. And as Intellect comes closest to the One, everything irradiated by Intellect bears witness to Unity. Hence Intellect is what links the world of phenomena with the Uncreated Creator and imbues all phenomena with the Truth. And these phenomena, being signs that point to Unity, can then become speech, for they bear the threefold seal of God, the Messenger and the Praised.

Unity reveals itself through multiplicity, and Peace through motion. Multiplicity and motion are contained in Unity and Peace, and vice versa. Everything which is multiple and in motion bears witness to the One. Thus every entity in the macrocosm and the microcosm is a sign created with the Truth; and every entity's innermost essence, i.e. that part of its being which is unbounded by space and time, is joined to Intellect through a chain of different planes of existence.

Man, too, as a sign, mirrors the attributes of his Creator. Thus it is no surprise that the poet's four names, received through no will of his own – *Mehmed* (i.e. *Muḥammad*), *Alija* (i.e. *'Alī*), *Muharem* (i.e. *Muḥarram*) and *Dizdar* – form a framework of signs that define his poetry, as do the symbols on the *stećci* and in the ancient books. The essence, however, which determines each sign is independent of form or language. The manifestations of signs in the outer world can be grasped by human reason, but their inner fullness can only be grasped by Intellect: for reason is the province of the brain, but Intellect the province of the heart. Openness to Intellect enables all signs in the macrocosm and microcosm to be matched with their archetypes in Intellect and thus to be translated into the fullness of Truth, where knowing and being are one and the same. When the myriad states of being are linked together in this way, the Word of God becomes recognised as the Message by which all of creation praises its Creator.

He who receives the fullness of this Message is the Messenger. He is known as *Muḥammad*, the Praised, for he shows in and through himself that 'praise belongs to God, Lord of the worlds'. His words and deeds are passed down as Tradition, renewing and confirming humankind's link with the Truth. The Praised is an interface between two seas, one fresh and one salt: the world of archetypes and the world of forms. Into the latter, i.e. the world of reason, he brings Intellect, and out of it he lifts the meaning of its signs onto a higher plane of being. Thus, through the example of the Praised, the descended ascends again. And the link between first and last, inner and outer, is to be found in the heart. Therefore the heart, as the interface between individuality and supra-individuality, the created and the Uncreated, is the Eye with which God sees Himself.

If every individual is a sign, we can only speak of individuality in terms of signs. The lower states in the chain of creation signify the higher states, with every sign on every plane of existence pointing to an archetype in Intellect. Thus all signs in the macrocosm can be deciphered when, via the Heart, they join their archetypes again.

> *'Alī*, the High, is the person closest in the world to the Praised. He is not the same as the Praised, for he is not an interface between two seas, but he knows the Praised and bears witness to him. Thus the High is humanity's example, the gate to the City of Knowledge. In the words of the Praised: 'I am the City of Knowledge and the High is its gate: therefore, whoever wants knowledge, let him learn it of the High.'[12]

Through the Praised, the real world is made sacred, for he forbids us to add to any sign's essence, or to subtract from it. Hence, in this world, man is *Muḥarram*: he who is 'under prohibition' or 'sacred'. The Man of Knowledge, realising this to be true for all the worlds, is he whose whole knowledge and being form a single answer to the question:

> Are you not aware
> how before God prostrate themselves
> all things that are in Heaven
> and all that are on Earth –
> the sun and the moon
> and the stars and the mountains
> and the trees and the beasts,
> and many of mankind?
>
> (Qur'an XXII:18)

Thus, wherever he may be, the Man of Knowledge knows he is in the Temple (*house, kuća, bayt; templum, hieron, masjid*). But the doors of the Temple, i.e. of the City of Knowledge, are constantly besieged by false knowledge, for some people deny Unity by idolising or denying the signified. Therefore he, the Universal Man, 'the Rightwise', is constantly fighting the wickedness of the world outside the Temple (*profanitas, tawajet*). This man is also known as the *Dizdar*, the Guardian of the City.

This, therefore, is an outline of the sacred science which illuminates the poetry of Muhammad 'Ali Muḥarram Dizdar. Independent of space or time, it can be expressed in any language. When man was expelled from Heaven because he had disobeyed the ban on the forbidden (*ḥaram*), sacred science receded, but it was not lost. Though this act darkened the individual's inner being, the darkness was never total; and if one learns to discern between the Real and the unreal, it can be swept away again. Man, 'cast out of Heaven', can link himself again (*religare*) to Heaven by following the Way which has been lowered to him like a lifeline.

4

Armed with insights from sacred science, we can now interpret the poet's signs in their true light. The Sun, which is the greatest Sign in the macrocosm, denoting access to Intellect within the totality of existence, has left deep and complex traces on Bosnian history:

> He rolled up his sleeves and ploughed the earth good
>   and deep
> right down to her bowels right down to her heart
>
> ('Sun')

The principle of the Sun, as reflected in Bosnia's written heritage, is the key to the relationship between *Stone Sleeper* and Sacred Tradition. Its most visible manifestation is the Book, which descends from God through His prophets. This descent is not a movement into the self from without, but the converse: the Book, its message already differentiated into speech or writing, goes out into the world from within, i.e. from the heart. And the white of the paper signifies the light of Intellect, infinite and eternal but made manifest through the written word.

The Perfect Man is he who is in direct contact with Intellect. He stands at the axis of the world, his plane of existence pierced by the Column of the Sun (a shaft of sunlight which corresponds to the seventh heaven, the seventh ray, the world behind the world). The Fallen Man, by contrast, has lost this contact, but there are ways in which it can be recreated. Though the traces left by the sign of the Sun risk being forgotten in the endless cycle of destruction and renewal, they are never completely effaced; in Dizdar's words, we are

> . . . still warming the whole of our soul
>
> By the heat of his long-gone golden hands
>
> ('Sun')

The duality between Perfect and Fallen Man reveals itself as a contrast between verticality, i.e. yearning for Unity, and horizontality, i.e. yearning for multiplicity. The former corresponds to the heart, and the latter to the brain. The relationship between them can be shown by the relationship between the Sun and the Moon: both are heavenly luminaries, but the latter only because it reflects the light of the former:

> What is true for the Sun and Moon is also true for the heart and the brain, or better for the faculties to which these two organs correspond and which they symbolise: that is, the intuitive intelligence and the rational or discursive intelligence. The brain, in as much as it is the organ or instrument of reason, truly plays only the role of 'transmitter' and, one might say, of 'transformer' [. . .] Intellectual intuition can be called supra-human, as it is a direct participation in universal intelligence which, residing in the heart, that is, at the being's very centre, where lies his point of contact with the Divine, penetrates this being from within, and illuminates him with its radiation.[13]

Light is the sign of knowledge. The light of the Sun represents direct knowledge, which derives from pure Intellect, while the light of the Moon symbolises reflected knowledge, which derives from the rational faculty and is therefore conditional and unstable. The poet says of the Moon:

> Carve his sign in the soft white of limestone
> so you may absorb as faithfully as can be

> The image of your infinite pain and hope
> ('Moon')

The true nature of knowledge is shrouded in mystery, and cannot be expressed by words alone. This does not mean its manifestations cannot be read, for it radiates through the human order according to strict laws. Only in the Heart, however, can knowing and being become one: outside this centre, which thought cannot penetrate, perception is blind to the true nature of its object.

Here the softness of limestone, in signifying the frailty of human existence and reason, also implies its opposite: the permanence of Mercy and Peace. *Pain* is the inevitable sensation as change begins, and *hope* is what follows as multiplicity turns into Unity. Thus reflected light, in bearing witness to its source, signifies the superiority of pure Intellect over its rational reflection. He who enables the reflection to rejoin its source, being to rediscover its archetype, is the 'Very Good' (Genesis I: 31), or the 'Praised'.

5

A person who is an interface between two seas or a bridge between two worlds, the supra-individual world of archetypes and the world of forms, has two aspects. The first is independent of individuality or language, but the second can manifest itself in any individual and language. The interface or bridge may take a host of names and shapes, different at each time and place, but it never betrays its prime, underlying essence.

But if we were to take a name or a shape – a prophet, say – to be the *only* manifestation, thus making the sign into more than it is, we would create a fatal divide between outer and inner worlds. Unguided by knowledge of Unity, we would lose our way in multiplicity. We might know of a road '. . . that comes / From left / Or / Right', that leads '. . . north / Or / South', through '. . . earth's roots where darkness has congealed', or '. . . from measureless heights'. But we would remain ignorant of the secret self, which is revealed only upon reaching the sea that lies beyond the six dimensions:

For you know least that in your life
The one true war
The hardest strife
Is at your very
Core

('Roads')

This desire for self-knowledge finds expression at every epoch and in every language. Its starting-point is confrontation with stone, with dead surface. Here the poet writes:

We need to become not stone
and eyes straight to walk unwavering through this stone
city's stone gate

('Rain')

The act of turning in fear towards the holy Temple, the Centre of the secret self, begins with knowledge of the *kolo*: the traditional South Slav round dance which, like the dance of the dervish monks, represents the whirling of the manifest forms around their timeless, spaceless Centre. Through the dance, the dancers can reach different stages in the realisation of individual existence. Three of these are critical. The first is identification with the centre of individual being, when forms merge with their supra-formal manifestations. The second is identification with the centre of all manifest states, formal and supra-formal, at the point where they merge with Universal Being. The third is identification with the Absolute, where an infinity of possibilities, manifest and non-manifest, merges with Supreme Reality.

This is signified in space by the cross, with man at its centre. Wherever and whenever he may be, space stretches outward before him into infinity; behind him, the direction signifies retreat, retraction. Similarly, space also stretches rightwards and leftwards, upwards and downwards. These three dimensions and six directions intersect and merge at a single point. Though it lies outside space, this is the starting-point of all development in space. It is symbolised by the Supreme Pen, the Seventh Ray and the Narrow Gate. It is attained by all individuals in whom past and future meet in an unbroken present. The act of linking the individual centre with the Centre, the individual present with Eternity, bears witness to the fact that there can be no truth but the Truth, and that there can be no I without the supreme I. In return for this release from the illusion of duality, 'truly we bear witness that Thou art!'

And so the gyring of the *kolo* around a single centre, as the dancers discover self through motion, corresponds to centripetal force, the pull of the centre, on an earthly plane:

> How long the kolo from hollow to hollow
> How long the sorrow from kolo to kolo
>
> Kolo to kolo from sorrow to sorrow
>
> ('Kolo of Sorrow')

From this Centre grows the vine. The vine and its branches signify harmonious growth and renewal, joining the world of six dimensions with the world which has its source in the Unity and Peace of the Seventh Heaven. Through the rhythm of ebb and flow, of inhalation and exhalation, the fullness of Unity is proclaimed in the worlds of being and conditionality. Thus the vine repudiates conditionality and bears witness to Unity.

> Present here is He
> Who said in faithful writ
> I am the true vine and my father is the husbandman and
> Every branch in me
> That beareth not fruit I shall take away
> But that the field wax fat the fruit be sweeter the root be
> deeper

The branch that beareth
I shall purge

Now ye are clean through the word which I have spoken
    unto you
Therefore cast ye your brute
Matter into this fiery flame Abide thus in me
And I most surely in you
As in those I abode in of old as in those whom I loved true

('The Vine and its Branches')

With these words, the Anointed restored, once and for all, the
covenant between created and Creator:

> I am the true vine, and my Father is the husbandman.
> Every branch in me that beareth not fruit he taketh away:
> and every branch that beareth fruit, he purgeth it, that it may
> bring forth more fruit.
> Now ye are clean through the word which I have spoken
> unto you.
> Abide in me, and I in you. As the branch cannot bear fruit
> of itself, except it abide in the vine; no more can ye, except
> ye abide in me.
> I am the vine, ye are the branches: He that abideth in me,
> and I in him, the same bringeth forth much fruit: for without
> me ye can do nothing.

(John XV: 1–5)

The Anointed's *I* is not a personal *I*, for He does not speak of
Himself. His *I* is the sign which leads to the Centre. It is the
relationship of the manifest and non-manifest with Intellect
and, through Intellect, with Unity. The Anointed has revealed
the Unity of the Centre through many of His testimonies:

> But when the Comforter[14] is come, whom I will send
> unto you from the Father, even the Spirit of truth, which
> proceedeth from the Father, he shall testify of me:

And ye also shall bear witness, because ye have been with me from the beginning.

(John XV: 26–27)

6

The poet's voice yearns for the gate of the City of Know-
ledge. The City represents man's presence on the earthly
plane. It enables us to distinguish between the market-place
and the vineyard, i.e. Earth and Heaven. Between the two
stands the narrow Gate:

> Here just guests we stand out still
> Although we should have crossed into a ring of light
> And passed at last through a strait gate in order to return
> Out of this naked body into the body eterne
>
> When I happened by this evening late
> Unbidden He said unto me
>
> I am that gate and at it enter into Me as I now into thee
> So He spoke but where is the mouth of the lock where
>   the finger of the one true key for the gate to the
>   burning stair?

('The Gate')

This is the call to the City. In one of many references to the
metaphor of the city and the gate or door, the Anointed said:
'I am the door: by me if any man enter in, he shall be saved'
(John X: 9). As for the Prophesied, who is the Praised and the
City of Knowledge, the Anointed testified that 'he shall not
speak of himself; but whatsoever he shall hear, that shall he
speak: and he will show you things to come' (XVI:13).

The Husbandman, God eternally one and the same, sum-
mons men to his vineyard: '. . . the kingdom of heaven is like
unto a man that is an householder, which went out early in
the morning to hire labourers into his vineyard' (Matthew

XX:1). The first day-labourers in the market place were hired at first light to start work at sunrise, but more were hired all day, right until the hour before sunset. Therefore 'the last shall be first, and the first last: for many be called but few are chosen' (XX:16):

> So forsake your father and mother forsake your sister and
>   brother
> Be loosed of this earth of ours and set ye no store by its
>   flowers
> Come out of the city by the east come out of her by the
>   west
> Build a city in thyself and turn thy face towards thy city
> For the time is at hand
>
> ('The Garland')

And so the one begins to gaze at the One, knowing that the signs in the outer world are the same as the signs in the self. But time is running out in order that the chosen might be saved. As the beginning grows ever more distant and the end ever closer, the divide between the market place and the vineyard becomes ever deeper and more marked. Multiplicity and motion, the attributes of the market place, obscure the outer world, making Unity and Peace, the attributes of the vineyard, seem ever more distant and dim. The gates of heaven seem ever more out of reach, and the signs ever more stridently denied. But those who close their ears to the din of the market place, who answer the Husbandman's summons, see all the more clearly the fate of the city that no longer knows the vine:

> In this world three powers shine three pillars of light stand
>   in a line
> Sun and Moon and the Perfect Man are the forces of the
>   macrocosm

He and the Virgin and Intellect in their midst are the
forces of the microcosm
The kingdom of heaven is inside us so let it be known
The kingdom of heaven is outside us
So let it be shown

('The Garland')

Though scattered through many manifestations, the creative
word is one. It is the source and rivermouth of everything.
And so the river of the world, that runs from death to life, can
be traversed by means of the Word: from dispersal in the
world one can travel back up to the source, but also down-
stream until it meets the sea. The act of waiting for the Word
to appear in the world guides one towards a new and primal
Radiance.

The Cross signifies Intellect as displayed in the world. In
Bosnian tradition, so powerfully reflected in Dizdar's poetry,
a host of examples bear witness to this sign. One example is
linked to Verses 6 and 7 of the Opening (Sura I) of the
Qur'an:

Guide us in the upright path,
The path of those whom Thou hast blessed,
not of those against whom Thou art wrathful,
nor of those who are astray.

The Cross's upper arm symbolises this upright path, i.e. the
steep path of Intellect and Spirit which leads upwards from
Earth to Heaven. It corresponds to the Column of Sun and
the Seventh Ray. Its lower arm symbolises the path of those
against whom God is wrathful: this is the downwards path
which leads from Earth to Hell, i.e. to the condition of soul
which is consumed in the heat of opposing its illusory will to
the Will of God. The horizontal arms represent entrapment
in the world: the path of those who have lost their way as
they stumble round in search of the Centre.

Another example is the testimony of Mary. When struck dumb by the slander of the lost, she pointed to her forehead, to her right and left shoulder, and then to her womb. Her sign has been interpreted thus: that which descends by the upright path from on high, from Intellect — as witnessed by the angel on her right and the angel on her left — to enter her womb is the Word of God and the Holy Spirit.

> But we have heard a new word
>
> Verily we have heard a word so new
> That be it but whispered the heavens ring
> A word which telleth of God's finger in the cross of the
>   Sun
> Of a city which shall be builded in us every one
> Of a vineyard and a husbandman
> Of a noble vine with stems which twine
> We have heard a word which tells of priests and unfading
>   garlands
> Of a gate that is strait before our weary feet
> We have heard the evil secrets of men in padded gowns
> We have heard of the bloody bed which the black
>   trackers have spread
> With cross and chalice with flame and baying of hounds
>
> ('BBBB', 5)

The myriad words return to the Word through the Praised — the bright lamp (Qur'an XXXIII:46), the shining example (XXXIII:21), through whom praise becomes manifest. He is the one of whom the Almighty said:

> My chastisement — I smite with it
> whom I will; and My mercy embraces all things, and
> I shall prescribe it for those who are conscious
> and pay the alms, and those who indeed believe
> in Our signs;

Those who follow the Messenger,
the Prophet of the common folk, whom they find
written down with them in the Torah and the Gospel,
bidding them to honour, and forbidding them
dishonour, making lawful for them the good things
and making unlawful for them the corrupt things,
and relieving them of their loads, and the fetters
that were upon them. Those who believe in him
and succour him and help him, and follow
the light that has been sent down with him –
they are the prosperers.

(Qur'an VII: 156–157)

The Praised speaks from the City within us, translating glory's signs into glory itself:

His speech was soft and warm like the welcome splash
Of spring rain in a parched plain
Through the thick black dark on the shore
Of a brackish sea and in the temple
On the road and on the olive hill
Where till that day no golden ray
No song of canny cock nor any choir

('BBBB', 8)

The speaker speaks not of himself. The words on his lips descended into his Heart from Intellect itself, in full submission to the One who is unlike any other, the incomparable:

Speaking so I told ye naught of myself
That which I said was my body and bread
From another I take that word which I spake
Yea I spake only the word
Of Him which speaketh
Through me

('BBBB', 10)

All the world and all of time bear witness only to Infinity and Eternity. All the roads of the world lead only towards individual extinction or the individual self; and the tales of those who travel these roads bear witness to what was in the beginning:

> (Walking the allotted way between the dark and the ray
> Walking the line of your sign
> Assailed by doubt
> And dismay
>
> I come back once more
> Crushed
> To the
> Core)
>
> ('BBBB', 12)

Self-knowledge, the only real insight gained from the waste-lands of the journey, becomes transformed into a prayer:

> (Lord
> Forgive me
> That I only arrived
> Back where I'd started so hopeful-hearted)
>
> ('BBBB', 14)

7

When unveiling the mysteries of Bosnia, the self meets a recurring image – the search for a House of Peace:

> Our Grandfathers' House was built to last
> In our hearts its strength
> Was meant to stand
> Fast
>
> ('House in Milé')

The House (*hiža, bayt, masjid, templum, hieron*) is a place where the covenant between God and Man may be renewed. This place can be anywhere on earth. When the Centre becomes present in the waking heart, it is unbounded by space or time: thus those who wake can make the Centre wherever they are. In so doing, they become a gate which opens on Heaven; and knowing the gate, they wait before it. They gain new life through the knowledge that dying in one state of being means rebirth in another: that every departure from this state means arrival in another. This is what is signified by the Door, the Narrow Gate, that leads to Heaven: the House is created in order to form a door to the Uncreated. And whoever has this Door in them becomes Uncreated, and therefore new (*novus, neos, navas*).

The House is the founding principle of the City, though it is not a principle in itself. In revealing the scope of fullness in contrast to emptiness, it is an extension of the Centre in the world of manifestations. Hence Unity is revealed through the myriad finite spaces and moments which the walls of the House enclose and unite. The House's outward diversity is a sign of the internal, unshakeable Unity by which it has its being. The powers that govern the House, from the immutable Centre which manifests itself in multiplicity, are temporal; but the authority above them, their guiding principle, is spiritual. And around this House, the City can take shape.

Breaking contact with the Centre and its manifestation in multiplicity leads to disintegration and disorder. As the link with Unity is lost, it becomes forgotten and withers away. The task of sacred science and sacred art, however, is to reveal Unity in multiplicity and return the individual to Unity through constant renewal of the Covenant. This renewal has two elements. The first is the act of distinguishing the Real from the unreal, and the second is the act of concentration on the Real. The first can be accomplished by all individuals, wherever and whoever they may be. But the second is non-individual and supra-individual. It derives directly from the Intellect, and demands purity of heart and insight into what is forbidden. This is the Way revealed by God through His chosen prophet, the Praised, the quintessence of all His prophets.

The Way, whose nature is always the same, though it can take many different forms, is received from the Messenger by the High. The High, by submitting himself utterly to supra-individuality, is a grandfather to others, caring and gentle, comforting and calm. He is also the first teacher after the Messenger, a master in the name of the One Who is Knowing and Wise. Through teaching others, he becomes a paradigm of submission, for nothing is his own: his freedom lies in obedience and trust, and in bearing witness, i.e. in doing what is beautiful and good. He hands on the testimony for his heir or heirs to keep as a sacred trust, as an ineffable mystery.

The earth is never without his heirs. Though they reveal themselves to the world, others see only their material exteriority or the light that pours from their inner selves. They dwell in that one Self where there can be no other, and their hearts are like bowls[15] into which the light of Intellect has been poured. They have 'come closer', for the Creator says of them:

> My slave keeps on coming closer to Me of his own free will till I love him, so I become his sense of hearing with which he hears, and his sense of sight with which he sees, and his hand with which he grips, and his foot with which he walks.[16]

And wherever there is an heir, a Grandfather, there is a House. A house without a Grandfather is not a House: it is but a place to wait until the promise is fulfilled. Only if there is a Grandfather can its doors be open for all.

The Grandfather, therefore, is the teacher, the Master through whom the Spirit, the link between knowing and being, is revealed. As the act of embracing the Real is passed down from the world of supra-individuality into the world of individual forms, transmission through a chain of masters ensures its presence in time. This chain links the Masters with the Prophet and thus with the single Essence of all Knowledge; and their own existence bears witness to this Knowledge. The earthly task of the Grandfather or Master, therefore, is to pass down the Prophet's spiritual message, to hand on the keys to the rites and sacred forms, and to give his pupils the lifeline of a link with Unity. The Master is aware of the relativity of such rites and forms, but also of their significance as a means of concentration on the Real. He follows only one form, but knows and acknowledges others. To him, the world of multitude and motion is like a wave-tossed sea. On its agitated surface one and the same Sun forms countless reflections. All its reflections are true. The Master knows their source, and the way which leads towards it; and on a calm surface, where fear, love and knowledge are resolved, reflection and source become one and the same.

Therefore the *House in Milé* is a place of mercy and peace for all who have turned towards the Centre. The name *Milé* invokes an ancient linguistic root which has given us the words 'mercy' (*milost*) and 'peace' (*mir*) in modern Bosnian. It can be found in various forms throughout Bosnia, testifying to a widespread wish to establish the covenant of Mercy and Peace:

> For welcome guests and passers-by
> And all whose hearts are
> Grand
>
> For all good people beneath the sky
> And all good folk in this Bosnian
> Land.
>
> For everich warryour in this mighty warre
> Which is now warring

On
Warre

On all other plagues and all
Other rogues
Great and
Small

('House in Milé')

They, the Grandfathers and those linked by them in a chain
to the Praised, also know of the false temples, the synagogues
of Satan[17], the mosques of opposition and unbelief,[18] where
lurk the persecutors of those who:

... yearned
For a sun that was big
And far away

('House in Milé')

They know about those 'who say: "We believe in God and
the Last Day"; but they do not believe' (Qur'an II: 8). They
know the Prophet's words: 'We are returning from a small
war to a mighty war'. They know the question: 'What is the
mighty war?'. They know his answer: 'The war against the
self'.[19] And they know not only about the mighty war, but
also about the Great Peace, which is attained when the heart
perceives Intellect as pure light. This Great Peace, revealed as
light, represents the Uncreated, and therefore the indestruc-
tible centre of the City. This – the actionless action of Unity
and Peace in the world of multitude and motion – is the
prime mover, the principle behind every temporal power.

They are alone, but in the world. They are present in multi-
plicity, but are joined to Unity. The words which describe the
House describe them too:

Let our Grandfathers' Great House
Stay open
Still

For all who do not care
For old
Or new
Tsars

For all who do not heed
Lordlings or kings or
Boyars

For all who do not need
Their wealth untold
Their evil gold
Their ducats
And their dinars

('House in Milé')

The doors of the House are open to the pure of heart. But where such hearts are lacking, there will be no such House. It will withdraw from the world, staying hidden until seen by new hearts:

But unless our Grandfathers' House be blest
By welcome stranger and guest
It will neither be mine nor thine
Nor our Grandfathers' House any more

('House in Milé')

8

Intellect, the column of sun which stands behind the myriad forms, transmutes worldly phenomena into signs. Acceptance of this fact enables one to turn towards the narrow or strait gate, of which the Anointed says: 'Enter ye in at the strait gate: for wide is the gate, and broad is the way, that leadeth to destruction, and many there be which go in thereat: Because strait is the gate, and narrow is the way, which leadeth unto life, and few there be that find it.' (Matthew VII:13–14). The same was said by the Praised: 'Those that cry lies to Our signs and wax proud against them – the gates of heaven shall not be opened to them, nor shall they enter Paradise . . .' (Qur'an VII:40)

In turning towards the gate, the seeker attains the purity of heart by which the self can be seen in the Self. Knowing then becomes the same as being, and the world becomes pure message. Accepting the Prophet means becoming like a branch on a vine, i.e. an extension and manifestation of Unity. Here there is no duality. Multiplicity fills emptiness, enabling Unity to be known to the self. The City is a plenitude where Peace becomes manifest through motion; and its precisest image is man, who was created in Peace's likeness. Thus the Absolute reveals itself in the conditional. It is known only to itself, through the Uncreated Heart. It is immovable and indivisible, but manifest in movement and multiplicity. It is present in every individual through the Centre, the founding Principle, and can be approached from all points of the compass.

But trying to enter the gate without a knowledge of the Centre and of the Uncreated, indestructible Principle within is a denial of the Spirit as Unity of knowing and being. This may destroy the Centre's manifestation in this world, but it cannot touch the Centre itself. Destruction, therefore, bears witness only to its own powerlessness in the face of Unity. As for the wasteland left in its wake, let us remember that:

> When thy goal liketh nigh
> Unto its desire –
> Know then
> That even his
> Body
> Was
> But
> A
> Moment's
> Home
>
> ('Message')

The message of *Stone Sleeper* is the denial of duality. The self as Absolute addresses the self as conditionality, and Unity becomes manifest. The self repeats Creation's primal sacrifice with the disordered and the impossible. The rite is one of transformation: what was once a macrocosmic descent becomes, through man, a microcosmic ascent. Heaven and Earth are drawn together and merge once more in Unity, through the speech of the indivisible, primal Unity that embodies the supreme Principle. A secret meeting takes place in the self between created and Uncreated, conditional and Absolute, finite and Infinite. Thus the Self, the supreme name, becomes a witness, and the witness merges with the Name which bears on nothing outside itself. The act of leaving the decay of the conditional world and returning to the self silences the unruly elements of the soul. Then, all obstacles removed, the soul can be urged and guided to rediscover its true nature as part of Reality, and man can build in himself a temple of the spirit. But the Fallen Man seeks his own downfall, in a bazaar of idols, a chaos of rationalisations, satanic imaginings, misdirected faculties of soul and inordinate attacks of desire and passion which have usurped his house and hold their carnival there.

Unity lies in the Self. Even suffering and destruction bear witness to Unity, for they symbolise a conditionality that has not yet come to consciousness:

> You know nothing . . .
>
> ('Message')

With the self's renewal in the Self as holy name, the House of the Heart is re-consecrated and the Holy Spirit, the Divine Breath, is revived. This House is the home of the Centre, the link with the Real; within it, man dwells in righteousness and justice, linked to Intellect and the Eternal.

It is not given to the individual to know the future. In 'Message', the last poem in *Stone Sleeper*, the division of Unity into *I* and *you* symbolises the relationship between the Absolute and the conditional. The world appears as conditionality, but points towards eternity, and memory of its original nature subverts the illusion of directness and non-conditionality. Thus the gathering pace of destruction only bears witness to the Final Hour, which has no dominion over the Uncreated. Error reaches its nadir in a host of abominations and a tyranny of numbers. Man is driven onto the lowest plane of the material world, losing his ability to discern between the unreal and the Real and hence his contact with the higher planes of Light. But error is still not all-pervading. The macrocosm is also sacred. Its conditionality must be proved in opposition to the Absolute, which means enduring an age of darkness. But the world cannot break its link with Heaven. Destruction of the City does not entail destruction of the Self: indeed, it confirms the self by its very conditionality. As the symbol of God, the world is circled with protection from human error. When movement reaches an apogee of darkness, it wheels round again, and a new cycle begins under the rule of Light. This is the intervention of Heaven, straightening out the deformities with which man has scarred the sacred face of Earth:

> No city is there, but We shall destroy it before the Day of Resurrection, or We shall chastise it with a terrible chastisement; that is in the Book inscribed.
>
> (Qur'an XVII:58)

But the end of the old cycle leads to a final separation between illusion, which is reduced to darkness, and the piercing light of the new cycle, which is embraced by the chosen. Thus, at the very end, balance is restored with the arrival of the Rightly-Guided, the Restorer who unites in himself the powers of Earth and Heaven. Meanwhile, as told in the Book of Revelation, the cycle of time gathers pace as it races towards its culmination. The macrocosm disintegrates in chaos, helpless and moribund, whilst the chosen embrace the Light of the new beginning. Thus the arrival of the Antichrist is, at the same time, the advent of the Restorer. The summons for the one is also the summons for the other:

So
Come on then
I've grown long used to your ravages
As if to the throes
Of a disease from far away

As to the icy waters swept savagely along
By this night river of darkness that grows
Ever more swift
And strong

('Message')

9

Stone Sleeper can only be properly understood once we understand its roots in sacred art and sacred science. The book's specifically Bosnian shape can be understood only in terms of the relationship between the Inner, which is always One and the Same, and the outer, which is manifested in multitude and motion. If removed from this context, the poet's voice is inarticulate, sowing only doubt and confusion. But if, by embracing and studying the book's underlying context, we attempt to bridge the gap between the temporal and the spiritual, Earth and Heaven, multiplicity and unity, then we may come a little closer towards the Centre. If not, the Centre will only become darker and ever more distant.

NOTES

1 See Šefik Bešlagić, *Stećci: Kultura i umjetnost [Stećci: Culture and art]*, Sarajevo, 1982; Marko Vego, *Zbornik srednjovjekovnih natpisa Bosne i Hercegovine [A Collection of Mediaeval Inscriptions of Bosnia and Herzegovina]*, I–IV, Sarajevo, 1962–1970; Marian Wenzel, *Ukrasni motivi na stećcima [Ornamental motifs on tombstones from Mediaeval Bosnia and surrounding regions]*, Sarajevo, 1965.

2 See Mak Dizdar, *Stari bosanski tekstovi [Old Bosnian Texts]*, Sarajevo, 1971; Kuna Herta, *Srednjovjekovna bosanska književnost [Mediaeval Bosnian Literature]*, Sarajevo, 1992.

3 On the history, doctrine and organisation of the Bosnian Church, plus other controversies associated with them, see Jaroslav Šidak, *Studije o 'Crkvi bosanskoj' i bogomilstvu [Studies on the 'Bosnian Church' and Bogumilism,* Zagreb, 1975; and Franjo Šanjek, *Bosano-humski krstjani i katarsko-dualistički pokret u Srednjem vijeku [The Bosnia-Hum krstjani and the Cathar-dualist movement in the Middle Ages*), Zagreb, 1975.

4 J. Morelli, *Codices manuscripti latini Bibliothecae Nonianae,*Venice, 1776, pp. 12–13.

5 Ibid.

6 Ćiro Truhelka, 'Testamenat Gosta Radina' ['The Testament of Gost Radin'], *Glasnik Zemaljskog muzeja [Gazette of the National Museum]* XXIII, Sarajevo, 1911, pp. 355–375.

7 See e.g. Ilarino da Milano, 'Fra Gregorio O. P. Vescovo di Fano e la *Disputatio inter catholicum et paterinum hereticum*', *Aevum XIV*, 1940, pp. 85–140.

8 *Archives of the JAZU*, Cyrillic Manuscript III, a, 41, fol. 31r–34 r.

9 Ivan Torquemada, 'Symbolum pro informatione manichaeorum', ed. N. Lopez Martinez–V. Proano Gil, *El bogomilisimo en Bosnia*, Burgos, 1958, p. 96.

10 Extract from Paul's Epistle to Titus (II:12–13), included in the *Manual of the Rites of the Bosnian Church*, written by Radoslav the 'Kristjanin' to the 'Kristjanin' Goisak, the original of which is preserved in the Vatican Library as *Manoscritto Borgiano Illirico*, 12, fol. 59.

11 For a fuller interpretation of this relationship see F. Schuon, *Gnosis: Divine Wisdom*, trans. G. E. H. Palmer, Middlesex, 1990, pp. 78–83.

12 Shaykh al-Mufīd, *Kitāb al-Irshād* (*The Book of Guidance into the Lives of the Twelve Imams*), New York, 1981, p. 21; Ibn Kathīr, *al-Bidāya wa'l-nihāja* (I–XIV), Cairo, 1351–8 / 1932–9, VII, p. 359.

13 René Guénon, *Symboles de la science sacrée*, Paris, 1962, p. 400.

14 In the Greek translation, the name *Parákletos* ('one called to the side of') is used, which is most often translated as *Advocate*, or *Comforter*. From earliest times, however, readings of this translation have suggested that the original word used was *Periklytos*, which corresponds in Aramaic – the language which Christ actually used – to *Mawhamana* ('The Much-Praised'), and to *Muhammad* in Arabic.

15 ʿAlī ibn Abī-Ṭālib said: 'These hearts are bowls. The best of them is the one which preserves. So preserve what I say to you [...] But the Earth is never devoid of those who maintain God's plea either openly and generally, or, being afraid, covertly, in order that God's pleas and proofs should not be rebutted.' (Nahj al-Balāghah: *Selection from sermons, letters and sayings of Alī ibn Abī-Ṭālib*, selected and compiled by As-Sayyid Abu'l-Ḥasan (Alī ibn al-Ḥusayn ar-Raḍī al-Mūsawī; trans. Syed Ali Raza, Tehran, 1980, pp. 688–689).

16 The Sacred Tradition as quoted in *Sahihul-Buhari*, Beirut, 1985, LXXVI:38.

17 'I know thy works and tribulation and poverty (but thou art rich) and I know the blasphemy of them which say they are Jews and are not, but are the synagogue of Satan.' (Revelation II: 9)

18 'And those who have taken a mosque in opposition and unbelief, and to divide the believers, and as a place of ambush for those who fought God and His Messenger aforetime...' (Qur'an IX:107)

19 This tradition is contained in al-Bayhakī, *Kitab al-Sunan al-Kubrà*, Haydarābād, 1344–55, *Kitāb al-zuhd*.

IVAN V. LALIĆ

Translated by Francis R. Jones

A Rusty Needle
The Passionate Measure
Fading Contact

'Although he has many lyrical poems on themes of love and landscape, the most distinctive part of his work relates to the ebb and flow of historical conquest and change on the northern shores of the Mediterranean.'

EDWIN MORGAN, *Poetry Book Society Bulletin*

'Poem after poem ignites in a virtuoso display of metaphor and image.'

GERARD SMITH, *Irish Times*

VASKO POPA

Collected Poems

Translated by Anne Pennington
Revised and expanded by Francis R. Jones
With an introduction by Ted Hughes

'Popa's imaginative journey resembles a Universe passing through a Universe. It has been one of the most exciting things in modern poetry, to watch this journey being made.'

TED HUGHES

'What makes these sequences so compelling is the sense that the ultimate riddle with which they are concerned is the riddle of life itself.'

DENNIS O'DRISCOLL, *The Times Literary Supplement*

VASKO POPA (ed.)

The Golden Apple

A Round of stories, songs, spells, proverbs and riddles

Chosen from 'Od Zlata Jabuka' and translated
by Andrew Harvey and Anne Pennington

'The book does much more than serve as background to the work of a fine poet. It is full of interest in its own right ... The contents range from concentrated versions of familiar fairy-tales – for instance 'the golden apple and the nine peahens' – to riddles, curses and proverbs. Throughout there is the sense of the unadorned, unrationalized essence of folk tradition ... This book entertains and startles afresh on each reading.'

MICHAEL CAYLEY, *PN Review*

'... an absolute delight. The tales fly along relentlessly to their enigmatic endings, mixing up the ridiculous, the miraculous and the commonplace, putting to shame the puerile moralizing of many modern children's books. The irrational is sitting in the trees waiting to leap upon you ... a marvellous Christmas present for any child whose sanity you wish to preserve.'

GEORGE SZIRTES, *Quarto*